PROPHET OF DISCONTENT

THE MOREHOUSE COLLEGE

KING

COLLECTION

SERIES ON CIVIL & HUMAN RIGHTS

General Editor

———

Vicki L. Crawford

THE KING COLLECTION

Advisory Board

———

Prophet of Discontent

*Martin Luther King Jr. and the Critique
of Racial Capitalism*

Andrew J. Douglas

Jared A. Loggins

THE UNIVERSITY OF GEORGIA PRESS

ATHENS

Library of Congress Control Number: 2020948819
ISBN: 9780820360164 (e-book: open access edition)
ISBN: 9780820360171 (hardback: alk. paper)
ISBN: 9780820360188 (paperback: alk. paper)
ISBN: 9780820360300 (e-book: standard edition)

CONTENTS

ACKNOWLEDGMENTS

This project began as an open-ended search in the Morehouse College Martin Luther King Jr. Collection. It has grown into a book that we hope will speak to a new era of movement activism. We made final revisions in the summer of 2020, as mass protests erupted in the United States and quickly spread worldwide. The tremendous groundswell of organizing energies, aimed at abolishing many of the same structural injustices that King fought against, breathed life into this book when the weight of the moment made writing especially difficult. We must first acknowledge those who have been killed, those who have been injured or jailed for protesting, and those who have taken to the streets in demonstration and have been lucky enough to return home unharmed, able to fight another day.

We owe a special debt of gratitude to Vicki Crawford, our Morehouse colleague who supported this project from its infancy and provided much-needed counsel as it matured. Many others in the Morehouse community have enriched our work: Sam Livingston, Kipton Jensen, Cynthia Hewitt, Frederick Knight, Matthew Platt, Adrienne Jones, Oumar Ba, Levar Smith, Lawrence Carter, Preston King, Patrick Darrington, and Jaeden Johnson. Beyond Morehouse, we owe thanks to Paul Taylor, Brandon Terry, Andrew Valls, Da'Von Boyd, Bryan Garsten, Lawrie Balfour, Ryan Russell, Justin Brooks, Jen Rubenstein, Dan Henry, Shaibal Gupta, Babak Amini, Meghnad Desai, Justin Rose, Ferris Lupino, De'Jon Hall, Michelle Rose, Gauri Wagle, and Paul Guttierez. Portions of the project were presented at the annual meeting of the African-American Intellectual History Society, the Yale Political Theory Workshop, the Brown University Graduate Political Philosophy Workshop, and the University of Virginia Political Theory Colloquium. We thank the participants in those discussions for their helpful queries and suggestions.

An earlier version of a portion of chapter three was the subject of the 2018 Frantz Fanon Memorial Lecture at the Asian Development Research Institute in Patna, India, and subsequently published as "King, Marx, and the Revolution of Worldwide Value," in *Karl Marx's Life, Ideas, Influences: A Critical Examination on the Bicentenary*, edited by Shaibal Gupta, Marcello Musto, and Babak Amini (New York: Palgrave MacMillan, 2019), 159-179. Another portion of chapter three, along with a small portion of chapter one, appeared in "Diagnosing Racial Capitalism," in *Fifty Years Since MLK*, edited by Brandon M. Terry (Cambridge: MIT Press/Boston Review, 2018), 40-44. We thank Palgrave and *Boston Review* for permission to republish this material.

At the University of Georgia Press, Walter Biggins, Lisa Bayer, and Nate Holly kept the project moving though personnel changes and the onset of a global pandemic. Two anonymous reviewers provided expert, and very timely, feedback.

And, of course, we thank our families: Marcie Dickson, and Juliana and Genevieve Douglas; Shari, Vernell, Justin Loggins, and Kimberly Wilson.

PROPHET OF DISCONTENT

CHAPTER ONE

"The Trouble Is ..."

On Critique and Tradition

The deep rumbling of discontent that we hear today is the thunder of disinherited masses, rising from dungeons of oppression.

—Martin Luther King Jr., *Where Do We Go from Here?*

The black revolution is much more than a struggle for the rights of Negroes.

—Martin Luther King Jr., "A Testament of Hope"

ON MARCH 27, 1968, a week before he was killed in Memphis, Martin Luther King Jr. joined Stanley Levison, Andrew Young, and several other confidants for an evening gathering at the New York City apartment of the singer and civil rights activist Harry Belafonte. Earlier that day, King had met with the poet Amiri Baraka in Newark, a city still reeling from the deadly riots of the previous summer. It was a city, King feared, that was poised to erupt all over again. At the time, King was working to organize the Poor People's Campaign, what was to be a multiracial march on and occupation of Washington, D.C.: a mass demonstration meant to press the American people into a serious confrontation with material poverty. And in New York that evening, King was in a "surly mood." He confided in Belafonte and others that Newark and his meeting with the militant Baraka had gotten to him, that suffocating conditions there and an increasing willingness among the city's youth to embrace violent resistance tactics were once again testing his long-haul strategy of nonviolent change. "I wholly embrace everything they feel," King said of the militant contingent in Newark. "I have more in common with these young people than with anybody else in this movement. I feel their rage. I feel their pain.

I feel their frustration. It's the system that's the problem, and it's choking the breath out of our lives."

As Belafonte recalls of the conversation that evening, it was Andrew Young—the future U. S. Congressman and Ambassador to the United Nations—who unwittingly ratcheted up King's anger. "I don't know, Martin," Young said. "It's not the entire system. It's only part of it, and I think we can fix that." King was having none of it. "I don't need to hear from you, Andy," he clapped back. "You're a capitalist, and I'm not. The trouble is that we live in a failed system. Capitalism does not permit an even flow of economic resources. With this system, a small privileged few are rich beyond conscience, and almost all others are doomed to be poor at some level. That's the way the system works. And since we know that the system will not change the rules, we are going to have to change the system."[1]

It was a striking conversation. Even more striking, perhaps, is that a similar conversation could have taken place among Black activists and organizers a half-century later. It could well have happened, for example, in July of 2014, when the system literally choked the life out of Eric Garner on Staten Island, or in August of that year, when the system cut down Michael Brown in Ferguson, Missouri, or in November of that year, when the system murdered 12-year-old Tamir Rice in Cleveland, or in April of the next year, when the system took Freddie Gray for one final "rough ride" through the streets of Baltimore. It could have happened in the spring of 2020, when the system once again choked the life out of a Black man, George Floyd, in Minneapolis, and deployed militarized police and posse units on Breonna Taylor in Louisville and Ahmaud Arbery in King's home state of Georgia. Fifty years after the system made a martyr of King, his thinking and perspective resonate in chilling ways. King was killed at a time when rage, pain, and frustration were widespread in American life, when the confluence of racial and economic inequity had set urban ghettoes aflame. Today, American cities teeter on the brink, and grassroots activists work to vivify the deadening vulnerability of Black lives. And as with King's era, as with the "long, hot summer" and its aftermath, today's unrest extends far beyond police brutality and state-sanctioned killings. "Today's insurgent black movements against state violence and mass incarceration call for an end to 'racial capitalism,'" Robin D. G. Kelley points out, and they take direct aim, Black Lives Matter co-founder Patrisse Kahn-Cullors says, at the "structural inequities" of a capitalist system that reproduces and enforces Black poverty and that has proven time and again to be incapable of loving, respecting, and honoring Black lives.[2]

In this moment it is worth revisiting King's indictment of capitalism. Recent scholarship has done much to recover King's radicalism, including his socialist commitments.[3] At a time when the language of democratic socialism is again moving more squarely into the public discourse in the United States, and in ways that resonate among a diverse cadre of young people, there is something to be said simply for acknowledging that one of America's revered national heroes espoused socialist and not capitalist ideals. But part of what is needed today is a more careful consideration of the material and intellectual constraints that prevent structural and behavioral change, that foreclose the realization of any socialist or substantively democratic future. Part of what is needed today is a sober and vivid account of the systemic and interconnected factors that contribute to the rage, pain, and frustration that King spoke of and that are still felt among so many. We argue that in this unfolding phase of the Black freedom struggle, an exposition of King's thinking about the entanglements of racism and capitalism can inspire and broaden the sort of systemic criticism that rarely works its way into the public discourse. The fact is that from his youthful engagement with anti-capitalist Christian theology and his initial reading of Karl Marx in 1949, King put himself into a lifelong "creative tension" with a wide-ranging critical theory of modern capitalism.[4] Though he is often cast as a dreamer or an idealist, his socialist aspirations are part of a rich and underappreciated diagnostic critique of capitalism's racial history and politics. King stressed that before we can know the cure, we first need an "accurate diagnosis of the disease."[5] This book sets out to expose and reconstruct key features of King's diagnostic critique of racial capitalism and to consider its contemporary applications—both its merits and its shortcomings.

To Kelley's point, many Black activists today, and certainly many in the scholarly community, call for an end to "racial capitalism." This language, which derives from the pioneering work of the late historian and political theorist Cedric Robinson, provides a generative opening for a renewed appreciation of King's thinking. In his seminal study of the Black radical tradition, Robinson argued that "the development, organization, and expansion of capitalist society pursued essentially racial directions, so too did social ideology," that "as a material force . . . it could be expected that racialism would inevitably permeate the social structures emergent from capitalism." Robinson used the term "'racial capitalism' to refer to this development and to the subsequent structure as a historical agency."[6] Though Robinson did not highlight King's critique of political economy—he focused primarily on an earlier generation of Black scholars, including W. E. B. Du Bois, C. L. R. James, and Richard Wright—King can be productively situated within this tradition, as a figure who factors the history of the Black liberation struggle into a creolized appropriation of Western intellectual legacies and who comes to regard institutionalized practices of capital accumulation as organically interwoven with racial domination, expropriation, and violence.[7]

The scholarship on King has not sought to elicit from his writings or speeches a coherent theory of racial capitalism or even a coherent theory of political economy.[8] Many of the more holistic biographical and historical accounts of King's life and work expose elements of a would-be theory: his religious and intellectual influences, his socialist sympathies, his engagement with labor politics, his efforts to mobilize in solidarity with the poor.[9] Our book addresses a gap in the theoretical literature. And it pushes beyond King studies to explore parallels with some of the contemporary scholarship on Black radicalism. We set out to reconstruct the critical theory of capitalist society that King's egalitarian vision requires. In this way, we read King in order to move beyond King. His unfinished work today requires a more critical dialogue about an abiding anti-Black racism and its maddening entanglements with the logic and practice of capital accumulation. This book is both an effort to carry on that unfinished work, however far we can take it, and a humble invitation for others to do the same. As prologue to that effort, we offer a brief exposition of the theory of racial capitalism and the Black radical tradition before turning to provide a prospectus of the study's four ensuing chapters.

Racial Capitalism

There are both historical and analytical dimensions to the theory of racial capitalism. Our application draws more heavily on the analytical, though it will be helpful to introduce both dimensions here, in part because together they underscore an intensely complicated relationship between Black radicalism and Marxist theory and politics. The latter, of course, has long been the conceptual lingua franca of the international anti-capitalist left, as well a common basis of comparison with King's economic thinking. Probably the most notorious attempt to draw such a comparison came from J. Edgar Hoover's FBI, which sought to paint King as a "whole-hearted Marxist."[10] Such an allegation was unfair and misleading, to say the least, but it warrants further exploration, especially for a study of the sort that we undertake here. The very tradition of a conventional or "whole-hearted" Marxism is part of what Robinson set out to complicate in his foundational account of the theory of racial capitalism.

In the Marxist tradition, the critique of capitalism took aim at several distinctive features of the capitalist mode of production, including private ownership of the means of production, the systemic and compulsory orientation toward ongoing capital accumulation and profit, and the institutionalization of a free labor market.[11] The *historical* dimension of the racial capitalism thesis sets out to complicate this latter feature and to conceive of racial expropriation, not as an outmoded relic of precapitalist feudalism, but rather as an integral component of the emergence and sustenance of capitalism itself. For Robinson, as Kelley neatly summarizes, "capitalism was 'racial' not because of some conspiracy to divide workers or to justify slavery and dispossession, but because racialism had already permeated Western feudal society. The first European proletarians were racial subjects (Irish, Jews, Roma or Gypsies, Slavs, etc.) and they were victims of dispossession (enclosure), colonialism, and slavery within Europe."[12] In Robinson's account, there were no capitalist societies, in Western Europe or on a more global scale, that were ever fully divorced from practices of racial division and domination. An indigenous European racialism, and the production and accumulation of economic value in and through practices of racial expropriation, was said to develop alongside the commodification of labor-power and the proliferation of contractually mediated labor relations.

This centering of race in an account of the emergence of the capitalist labor regime is, to be sure, an affront to conventional Marxist wisdom. Marx, for his part, was attentive to racism and he took very seriously the horrors and world-historical significance of the transatlantic slave trade.[13] "In actual history," he wrote in *Capital*, "it is notorious that conquest, enslavement, robbery, murder, briefly force, play the great part."[14] But Marx built his theory of capitalism largely on the established presuppositions of nineteenth-century European political economists, including what he acknowledged to be their "idyllic" notion of a sort of racially blind capitalism, a stripped-down model of an economy based exclusively on the exploitation of nominally free wage-labor. Marx sought to disclose an exploitative process built into the "silent compulsion" of market relations, and he relegated racial and other allegedly extra-economic modes of expropriation to a phase of what he called, following the bourgeois economists of the period, the "so-called primitive accumulation" of capital. In taking the nineteenth-century political economists to task on their own terms, in trying to show that the institution of a free labor market would lead not to rising tides and the proliferation of democratic freedoms, but rather to unsustainable inequalities between exploited producers and an ownership class, Marx struggled to register the ways in which racism and racial domination had been woven into the workings of mature capitalist societies. Some 150 years after the publication of *Capital*, Achille Mbembe points out, "capital not only remains fixed in a phase of primitive accumulation but also still leverages *racial subsidies* in its pursuit of profit."[15] This sobering observation, common to an increasing number of scholars and activists today, is often taken as ample testimony that, when it comes to race, Marx simply missed the mark.

Following the sociologist Oliver C. Cox, who argued that Marx relegated "as subsidiary the very things which should have been the center of his study," Robinson and subsequent theorists and historians of racial capitalism have sought to foreground the persistence of racial violence and expropriation within the divisions of labor and relations of exchange that capital accumulation requires.[16] A centering of the histories of racism and enslavement in the making of the capitalist world system enables fuller appreciation of both "capitalism's commodification of the human" and the ongoing "reworking of slavery."[17] Concerns about the development of more complicated modes of human commodification and semi-commodification—more complicated ways in which human beings are put into servitude—were absolutely central to King's critique of postwar capitalist society. "We still have slavery," he said bluntly in 1962, "slavery covered up with certain niceties of complexity."[18]

It is important to keep in mind that Marx, for his part, moved between historical and analytical registers. This slippage is part of what has led to so much ambiguity about the legibility of race and racism within his theory of capitalism as well as the extent to which a sharper and more consistent attentiveness to race can be rendered consistent with it. King's reference to a modern-day slavery, to a brand of servitude "covered up with certain niceties of complexity," points toward at least one way in which the *analytical* dimension of the theory of racial capitalism reflects not a rejection of Marxist thought, but rather an expansion of it.

Part of what distinguished Marx from other critics of his time, and part of what might help to explain Marx's ambivalence about slavery and "the so-called primitive accumulation" of capital, was his attempt to account for the tendency toward *impersonal* domination and exploitation. Under conditions of formal slave labor, and especially within regimes of modern racial slavery, it is easier to identify perpetrators and to assign accountability or blame for outwardly unjust relationships between human groups. The task of identifying and assessing responsibility, of gleaning a sense of who does what to whom, is more difficult under the impersonal structure of a society in which human relations, including labor relations, are more fully and regularly mediated by market exchange.

Nancy Fraser reminds us that "Marx looked behind the sphere of exchange, into the 'hidden abode' of production, in order to discover capitalism's secrets"—in order to show how exploitation and inequality are themselves reproduced under the capitalist mode of commodity production. This move, surely, has proven to be immensely revelatory, in Marx's day and well into our own. But, as Fraser goes on to argue, in order to further develop "conceptions of capitalism and capitalist crisis that are adequate to our time," we need to "seek production's conditions for possibility behind that sphere, in realms still more hidden."[19] We need, she says, an "expanded conception of capitalism," one that goes beyond an analysis of capitalist *economy* to include also an account of "capitalist *society*," or the "background conditions" that enable and sustain the production and circulation of value. And as Michael Dawson has argued, one such necessary background condition is precisely the "'hidden abode of race,'" or "the ontological distinction between superior and inferior humans—codified as race—that was necessary for slavery, colonialism, the theft of lands in the Americas, and genocide," and that "produced and *continues to produce* the boundary struggles" characteristic of capitalist expropriation.[20]

As Jodi Melamed reminds us, "capital can only be capital when it is accumulating, and it can only accumulate by producing and moving through relations of severe inequality among human groups." Such accumulation, she says, "requires loss, disposability, and the unequal differentiation of human value," and "racism enshrines the inequalities that capitalism requires."[21] Throughout the book, in our reading of King, we are mindful of how racial differentiations and inequities are presupposed by and reproduced systematically in and through processes of capital accumulation. We show how, in his later years especially, as he pressed harder on the capitalist "structure of society," on a "total pattern of economic exploitation," on a "capitalistic system predicated on exploitation, prejudice, [and] poverty," King moved toward precisely the expanded conception of capitalist society that Fraser and Dawson explicate: a capitalist society enabled by the "hidden abode of race."[22]

To recover these aspects of King's critical theory is to expand appreciation of his critique of racism. At his best, we argue, King helps to debunk what Adolph Reed has decried as "arresting but uninformative and strategically useless metaphors, such as the characterization of racism as a 'national disease' or the chestnut that racism 'takes on a life of its own' or other such mystifications." And here, to be sure, our study cuts against conventional readings of King. He is often remembered principally as a soaring orator and an accessible public communicator, the mass mobilizer of the mainstream civil rights movement. In this way, he is often caricatured as precisely the sort of figure who trafficked in the very mystifications that Reed warns about. As Reed goes on to point out, "racism is not an affliction; it is a pattern of social relations. Nor is it a thing that can act on its own; it exists only as it is reproduced in specific social arrangements in specific societies under historically specific conditions of law, state, and class power."[23] Part of our effort to recover from King's work a critical theory of racial capitalism is to show that King—the frequently "sanitized" civil rights icon—provides a far more generative way of thinking about sources of persistent racial injustice and what it will take to really challenge the system.

It is important to emphasize, too, what we might call the "necropolitical" aspect of the theory of racial capitalism, or the ways in which capitalist societies rely upon and reproduce not only economic exploitation, but also "logics of elimination or genocide," or what Jackie Wang refers to as a "logic of disposability."[24] And here again, the Marxist tradition provides a useful foil. The key point is that the projects of racial formation that enshrine the unequal differentiation of human value and normalize background conditions are at once independent of capitalism but service capital accumulation. Dawson has suggested that a "colonial logic" operates alongside an accumulative economic logic. And, he points out, "the process of expropriation marked by colonial logics is different from that described in traditional Marxist analyses due to its racialization. The colonial logic of superior/inferior human includes not only ongoing expropriation and exploitation, but disposability, and an attenuated extension of citizenship or subject 'rights,' if they are extended at all. Racially expropriated labor never becomes 'free labor' in the classic Marxist sense."[25] One of King's persistent concerns was that the capitalist drive for technological innovation, and principally the automation of labor and the displacement of jobs, had and would continue to have devastating effects on Black lives and livelihoods. In this King clearly anticipated what have become grave contemporary concerns about capitalist production of a Black surplus population and the disposability of Black lives, which today's prison abolitionists and the activists involved in the Movement for Black Lives, among others, continue to work so courageously to disclose and confront. Today, Kali Akuno says, "Black life is a commodity rapidly depreciating in value" and is "becoming increasingly more disposable." As the capitalist system struggles to "absorb dislocated and displaced populations into productive endeavors," we find ourselves staring down an "era of correction and contraction that will have genocidal consequences for the surplus populations of the world if left unaddressed. The Black working class is now confronting this genocidal threat."[26] King said in 1966 that the "ultimate logic of racism is genocide," and there is no question that a colonial logic of racial exploitation, expropriation, *and disposability* undergirds his mature critique of the capitalist world system.[27]

The Black Radical Tradition

One upshot of this theoretical approach is that it suggests a way around the race-versus-class impasse that has historically hampered coalitional movement building. If capitalism relies upon the maintenance of a racial order, if racialized background conditions normalize and routinize the unequal differentiations of human value that capital accumulation requires, then it would follow that when the racial order crumbles, the logic of capital accumulation will be undermined. The conditions that enable the production and circulation of value will be compromised. To fight racism and structures of racial domination and expropriation, then, is not to deflect attention away from the class struggle, or to prioritize cultural or superstructural concerns over material ones. It is to attack a structural pillar of distributive injustice. It is to act on the sobering recognition that, as Malcolm X put it in 1964, "you can't have capitalism without racism."[28]

This is a striking line from Malcolm X. King never made the connection in quite so stark a way, at least not publicly, which raises questions about whether or not more avowedly radical strands of twentieth-century Black thought—the ideas and perspectives behind the postwar Black nationalist or Black Power movements, for instance—might provide a more apt basis for a study of this sort.[29] If one looks, for example, at the cooperative movement unfolding today in Jackson, Mississippi, the "most radical city in America," one sees the critique of racial capitalism on full display, and one sees not the civil rights legacy of King and the Southern Christian Leadership Conference, but rather the more militant nationalist legacy of Chokwe Lumumba and the Provisional Government of the Republic of New Afrika, the work of the New Afrikan People's Organization and the Malcolm X Grassroots Movement.[30] It would be a scandal to suggest that King is somehow a more fitting intellectual forebear to the struggles unfolding today in a place such as Jackson, or to suggest that King occupies some sort of privileged mantle in the long and complex history of the critique of racial capitalism. But that critique is there in King, surely, and to provide a fuller exposition of it is to expose a more radical King, one who perhaps ought to be recast in the popular and scholarly imagination as part of a broader coalition of Black radicalism. Here again Robinson's work—in particular, his expansive conception of a Black radical tradition—provides a useful frame of reference.

Robinson described the Black radical tradition as "an accretion, over generations, of collective intelligence gathered from struggle." It began in slavery, he said, "in the daily encounters and petty resistances to domination—"struggles through which "slaves had acquired a sense of the calculus of oppression as well as its overt organization and instrumentalization." Over generations, "the rationale and cultural mechanisms of domination became more transparent. Race was its epistemology, its ordering principle, its organizational structure, its moral authority, its economy of justice, commerce, and power." Gradually the "tradition was transformed into a radical force, and in its most militant manifestation, no longer accustomed to the resolution that flight and withdrawal were sufficient, the purpose of the struggles informed by the tradition became the overthrow of the whole race-based structure."[31]

Again, for Robinson, the whole race-based structure was and is racial capitalism. And to document a tradition oriented toward its overthrow, indeed to consider that tradition's self-activity, is to expose and work from the racial myopia of conventional European radicalism. As Avery Gordon has argued, "the Black radical tradition stands not simply as a colossal example of a blindspot in the Marxist point of view. Rather, the Black radical tradition stands, living and breathing, in the place blinded from view; it is, in the deepest sense of the term, a theoretical standpoint and not merely a set of particular data."[32] At issue, in other words, are not merely factors of analysis or data points, not only the question of how many Black lives are taken by the police—as desperately important as that question is—but also, crucially, a theoretical standpoint born of Black lives. And again, the kneejerk reaction to dismiss this theoretical standpoint as a distraction from or even a threat to the class struggle remains a real problem.

David Roediger has pointed out that nowadays, several decades into the devastating neoliberal assault on both labor and antiracism struggles, it makes sense to return to King's era, to the 1950s and 1960s, for this was an instructive time, "a period in which the permeability of race and class emerged in sharp relief." It was a period in which "the expanding horizons created by the movements against racial oppression made all workers think more sharply about new tactics, new possibilities, and new freedoms. The spread of wildcat strikes across color lines is one example. The high hopes Martin Luther King Jr. invested in both the Poor People's Campaign and the strike of Black sanitation workers in Memphis remind us of a period that could test ideas in practice and could experience, if not always appreciate, the tendency for self-activity among people of color to generate possibilities for broader working-class mobilization."[33]

So, Robinson's idea of the Black radical tradition—which, it must be said, is not an uncontested category—provides a broadly generative framework for thinking about King's critique of racial capitalism.[34] Three aspects of this tradition, in particular, shape our reading. The first is precisely this abiding emphasis on indigenous Black struggle, the self-activity of a people. Though King is frequently held up as an exemplary leader of the masses, a "great-man" hero par excellence, we follow recent civil rights historiography that has sought to complicate, if not correct, this common simplification. We explore some of the ways in which King's thinking and activism, like those of other recognized personalities of the movement, were shaped by the self-activity of the people. This is not to diminish King's stature or genius as a mobilizer. Nor is it to imply that King was exemplary in his responsiveness to a more implicit leadership carried out by the rank and file. His thinking about patriarchy and heteronormativity, to cite two glaring examples, certainly should have—and had he lived, perhaps would have—taken cues from Black feminist and queer perspectives, from the lived expressions of how these structures of power and domination, among still others, shape the background conditions that enable capital accumulation.[35] Still, as this chapter's opening reference to King's response to the youth in Newark attests, King's thinking about race and capitalism would have been nothing without direction from below.

A second aspect involves an orientation toward violence, including an antipathy toward property ownership as a form of structural violence. In his account of the "character," or "the ideological, philosophical, and epistemological natures of the Black movement," Robinson highlights a distinctive attribute that "was always there, always indicated, in the histories of the tradition. Again and again," he says, "in the reports, casual memoirs, official accounts, eye-witness observations, and histories of the tradition's episodes, from the sixteenth century to the events recounted in last week's or last month's journals, one note has occurred and recurred: the absence of mass violence." Often to the amazement of Western observers, "Blacks have seldom employed the level of violence that they (the Westerners) understood the situation required."[36] This is a sweeping historical assessment, certainly, and a complicated philosophical matter. "There was violence of course," Robinson is keen to emphasize. But his key points, which resonate deeply with King's practice and philosophy of nonviolence, and also help to expand our appreciation for how King's orientation toward violence interweaves with his economic critique, are that the violence of the resistance has always paled in comparison to the preemptive and reactionary violence used to established and maintain "capitalist slavery and imperialism" past and present, and that there is a profound philosophical significance to this. For Robinson, this history reflects "a renunciation of actual being for historical being," a negation of the lived realities of racial capitalism and an affirmation—or what he calls the "preservation," however imagined or conjectural—of an Africana sensibility that "had never allowed for property in either the physical, philosophical, temporal, legal, social, or psychic senses."[37] At issue is an indictment, in racial and civilizational terms, not only of an economic system predicated on commodification of the human and private ownership of the means of production, but also of a broader cultural liberalism, a long-established Western social and political rationality for which claims to ownership, an instinct to demarcate between what belongs to one individual or party and not to another, reflect a violent foreclosure of the very possibility of sociality, of being and living together, indeed of the "beloved community" that King imagined.

This points toward a third aspect that informs our study, which is perhaps an amalgamation and extension of the first two. It has to do with how we think about politics and the political. From his earliest work, Robinson sought to trouble the prevailing rationality of Western authority, its very "terms of order."[38] He took issue with the ways in which a mythos of leadership, and the normalization of rigid hierarchies and an intellectual and material elitism, had been reinforced by industrialization and the consolidation of capitalist society. What became for Robinson the Black radical tradition, in particular its gesturing toward a "whole other way of being," was conceived more narrowly in his earlier political science work as "an *antipolitical* tradition." He spoke of a contrast between "political and nonpolitical societies, that is those societies in which there was an attempt to contain power by routinizing or institutionalizing it and those societies in which this question did not arise."[39] This contrast is helpful. It helps to trouble both the racial capitalist world that we occupy, political as it most surely is, and the very status of the political in King's work. To many, as we have noted already, King was and remains an embodiment of a Western conception of leadership. And in his public pronouncements anyway, he never gave up on the idea that the Western model of the territorial nation-state could be salvaged as a vehicle for righting the wrongs, racial and otherwise, that it had been set up to propagate and institutionalize. But King was also a deeply imaginative thinker, one whose dreamy, even utopian visions for new ways of working, living, and loving together require real sacrifice, if they stand any chance of coming into being. And such sacrifice includes, surely, the abandonment of familiar conceptions of politics and the political, of leadership and authority, of the very terms of the racial capitalist order.

Prospectus

These considerations, very much grounded in Robinson's work, course through this book and inform our reading of King. In chapter two, we set out to reconstruct King's critical methodology and to consider how theory as such helps people make sense of and evaluate their world, how theoretical and historical narratives help to contour and structure lived experiences. Through an exploration of King's Christian theological influences and his embrace of the dialectical legacy of Hegel and Marx, we show that King's critical imagination was shaped early on by what we call a redemptive narrative structure. This narrative structure gives King a prefigured confidence in the need to reconcile tensions or contradictions that can be exposed in the world, and this structure is central to his later critique of the internal contradictions of racial capitalism. The chapter also considers King's status as a critic of ideology—that is, the false or illusory perceptions that give legitimacy to the established order. King was a formidable critic of established wisdom, certainly, but his criticism of ideology went beyond this. We try to fill out a more comprehensive picture by showing that his dialectical emphasis on tension and conflict trains focus on social relations that are hidden or secreted away not only by the biased or distorted claims of ideological consciousness, but also by the very nature of commercial society. King's critical theory can be said to push beyond the epistemic, out to the terrain of the ontological, to a critical confrontation with what Cedric Robinson has called the "actual being" of racial capitalism. By exposing this more radical dimension of King's methodological apparatus, we are better able to see how King put himself into critical contact with racial capitalism's underside—what he called "the other America"—and we are able to grapple more seriously with his diagnostic critique of the "structure of the economy" as well as his political movement toward a radical "restructuring of the whole of American society."

In chapter three—which is a more ambitious and exploratory chapter, and in many ways the heart of the book—we consider how King's well-known call for a "revolution of values" is complicated by the production and circulation of value in capitalist society. Here we are concerned principally with how the coordination of human labor and activity, the kinds of human interdependencies that King referred to as the "inescapable network of mutuality," have become sustained in the modern world by the logic of capital accumulation—that is, a distinctive pressure put upon market actors to pursue not only profit, but also sustained growth through the creation of viable outlets for reinvestment. What we are compelled to value and devalue in capitalist society is largely dependent upon its movement through cycles of accumulation and reinvestment. And this movement is itself dependent upon the reproduction of social inequalities, which have significant temporal and spatial dimensions, as well as discernible racial dimensions. We show how King's attunement to these dynamics was shaped by his conscription into the movement in Montgomery in the mid-1950s and by his exposure to a burgeoning Black internationalism into the mid-1960s. King's readers frequently underappreciate the extent to which his mature antiwar arguments were interwoven with and bolstered by a sophisticated analysis of capitalist imperialism—that is, by the production and circulation of value in the capitalist world system.

King's critique was a product of its era. But in many ways its explanatory power transcends its historical genesis and speaks quite productively to Black resistance struggles into the neoliberal age. We pick up with this theme in chapter four, where we reckon with the layered nature of King's political theory and situate King's critique of capitalism more squarely within an ongoing Black radical tradition. In one sense, King's critique of capitalism, both its diagnostic and more prescriptive aspects, remained wedded to a rather conventional, state-centered conception of the political. His calls for capital controls, expanded welfare programs, and other government provisions and regulations were befitting of an era of state-managed capitalism. But King was never interested in empowering the state, which he understood to be an apparatus of repression and control. The idea was always to empower communities, the publics that states could be made to serve. We argue that his speculative pursuit of the "beloved community," a concept born of the communal nature of the Black freedom struggle, reflects a movement to fashion more imaginative ways of living, more democratic ways of being together that are not circumscribed by the dominion of racial capitalism and its apparatuses of governance and control. Insofar as capitalism's state-managed phase has, since King's death, given way to a neoliberal era—one in which the private power of global capital has more thoroughly captured territorial state power worldwide and dramatically undermined the welfare state contract—King's emphasis on community organization, the cultivation of what we call the Black counterpublic, speaks to the realities of our time.

This claim warrants further discussion, which we undertake in chapter five, of the afterlives of King's critique. The King Memorial Center (later the King Center for Nonviolent Social Change), established shortly after King's death, has been the most prominent institutional steward of the King legacy. But in 1970, Vincent Harding and several other prominent Black scholar-activists broke from the King Center and established the Institute of the Black World

(IBW), an international think tank that, in many ways, was meant to carry on the more radical aspects of King's intellectual and scholarly work, including its anti-capitalist and Pan-African dimensions. Building on the work of the historian Derrick White, we offer a case study of the IBW.[40] While it was relatively short lived, shuttered by the early 1980s, the IBW provides some indication of the kind of institutional space that could facilitate the critique of racial capitalism into the twenty-first century. In contrast to other Black civil society institutions of the post–civil rights era—such as the Joint Center for Political and Economic Studies (JCPES), which was more keen to work within liberal democratic institutions and promote the interests of a burgeoning Black political class—the IBW focused on a form of Black studies and global scholar-activism that was not reducible to what Robinson calls the Western "terms of order." Today there is a call to renew and expand Black studies, and very deliberately as an enterprise to be carried out independently of the strictures of established institutions, including traditional colleges and universities. By reconstructing the critical theory of capitalist society that King's vision requires, by exploring the institutional spaces that have facilitated and might again be made to nurture this kind of work, we hope to amplify and enrich that call.

Throughout these chapters, we employ a presentation strategy that allows us to survey aspects of King's critique in a way that is deliberately inexhaustive and that, we hope, will be conducive to further study. Each chapter is loosely anchored by reference to one of King's theoretically significant texts—or, in the case of the final chapter on the afterlives of King's critique, an essay by Vincent Harding. In each chapter, we identify and parse out significant phrases or passages as a means of organizing the discussions. This approach reveals that certain themes, concerns, principles, and phrasings course through King's writings and speeches and lend themselves to the reconstructive efforts we undertake. But like Robinson, who in his study of the Black radical tradition said that his "purpose was never to exhaust the subject, only to suggest that it was there," we recognize that there is so much more to be discovered, reconstructed, and debated about King and the critique of racial capitalism.[41] Surely there are additional stories to be told about King's anticapitalism, perhaps ones that build on our work but that foreground his Christianity and religious commitments, for example, or that mine his business sense or personal financial affairs, much more than we do.

All told, this book attempts to complicate King's legacy and elevate his struggle for a better world. In 1967, in his famous antiwar speech in New York City, King said that "there is nothing except a tragic death wish to prevent us from reordering our priorities so that the pursuit of peace will take precedence over the pursuit of war. There is nothing to keep us from molding a recalcitrant status quo with bruised hands until we have fashioned it into a brotherhood."[42] But surely the obstacles, from ideological and fetishistic obfuscation to the emboldened interests of counterrevolution, are far more formidable, far more complex, than King let on from that Morningside Heights pulpit. This, of course, King knew all too well. In the last years of his life especially, King battled through fits of depression, a recurring sense that in trying to organize the poor, in trying to restructure the edifice of a world economy that churns out beggars, he was chasing something of a fool's errand. Many in his inner circle, including veteran anti-capitalist soldiers such as Bayard Rustin and Stanley Levison, sought to persuade King that the United States was just not yet ready for radical political-economic restructuring. And yet King soldiered on. Part of what he gave us, in the last years especially, was a compelling critical theory, a diagnostic account of racial capitalism. This was no fool's errand. Perhaps now more than ever, King's critique can help to motivate incisive thinking about the obstacles that foreclose realization of a more just world.

CHAPTER TWO

"The Other America"

On the Method of Dissatisfaction

> I need not remind you that poverty, the gaps in our society, the gulfs between inordinate superfluous wealth and abject deadening poverty have brought about a great deal of despair, a great deal of tension, a great deal of bitterness.
>
> —Martin Luther King Jr., "The Other America"

> We have a task, and let us go out with a divine dissatisfaction.
>
> —Martin Luther King Jr.,
> Speech at the 11th Annual SCLC Convention

T OWARD THE END OF his life, King began to speak of "literally two Americas." One, he said, was "flowing with the milk of prosperity and the honey of equality" and was the "habitat of millions of people who have food and material necessities for their bodies, culture and education for their minds, freedom and human dignity for their spirits." The other "has a daily ugliness about it that transforms the buoyancy of hope into the fatigue of despair." King would go on to say that "probably the most critical problem in the other America is the economic problem."[1] As we work up a diagnosis of the economic problem, it will be helpful to establish some methodological context. What does it mean for King to expose "the other America"? How did he bring himself into critical contact with racial capitalism's underside? In what ways did he court and counsel his sense of dissatisfaction?

King was, of course, a public intellectual and a prominent social critic. The arc of our treatment of this dimension of his life and work begins with an attempt to situate his methodological apparatus within a tradition of modern

critical theory, broadly understood. Ultimately, King exceeded the terms of
Western critical theory, and in ways that are quite telling for how we might
understand and wrestle with the lived realities of racial capitalism into our own
time. But we begin with a figure engaged in what James Tully calls "public philosophy as a critical activity" or what a young Karl Marx referred to simply as
the "self-clarification of the struggles and wishes of the age."[2] The idea is that
meaningful social and political theorizing does not detach itself from the lives
and struggles of ordinary people, but is, rather, a kind of "methodological extension and critical clarification" of the practical reasoning that historically situated actors always already engage in.[3] Most of us work very hard to make sense
of our situation in the world. We try to provide satisfying reasons for why we
think and behave as we do. We try, and often struggle greatly, to communicate
and coordinate our thoughts and behaviors with others. In a very fundamental
sense, this sort of practical reasoning is what public life is all about. King, for
his part, worked toward a methodological extension and critical clarification of
the struggles and wishes of "the other America." He sought to model a public
intellectualism in service of a Black radical counterpublic.[4] And yet, and this is
really the overarching claim of this chapter, King cultivated a methodological
approach that revealed just how difficult this task can be, a difficulty owing in
large measure to the very nature of the economic problem as King was able to
apprehend it.

One reason to situate King within a tradition of modern critical theory,
at least initially, is that King fashioned himself as a dialectical thinker, and
a Hegelian of sorts. As such, King was equipped to home in on the complex
interrelationships that sustain the social, political, and economic order. He was
able to see clearly the ways in which the "two Americas" are interdependent
and condition one another. He was able to vivify societal conflict and tension,
the internal contradictions of racial capitalist modernity, and he was able to
do so in ways that motivate and sustain not only a critical judgment of a con-
tradictory historical order, but also a collective movement toward historical
reconciliation. For us, the signal upshot of recovering King's indebtedness to
the dialectical tradition is that it enriches appreciation of King's role as a critic
of ideology. It enriches a sense for how King exposed the political motivations
behind the ideas and values and structural logics that give legitimacy to the
established order.

There is no question that King was, as Vincent Lloyd puts it, "suspicious of the
wisdom of the world, ideology." He sought to expose and challenge the dominant ideas and values that obscure unequal social relations—what Lloyd calls the

"mystification used by the powerful and wealthy to secure their own interests."[5] But here again King worked toward a broader intellectual radicalism than is often acknowledged. We fill out a more comprehensive picture of King's critical methodology by showing that his dialectical emphasis on tension and conflict trained focus on social relations that are hidden or secreted away, not only by the "wisdom of the world," not only by the biased or distorted claims of ideological consciousness, but also by the very nature of commercial society. King's critical theory pushes beyond the epistemic, to the terrain of the ontological, to a critical confrontation with what Robinson has called the "actual being" of racial capitalism.[6]

Throughout the chapter we draw on the 1968 iteration of King's "Other America" speech in order to broach and work through several themes relevant to our discussion. As a pastor and public intellectual, as a figure who traveled widely and delivered sermons and speeches over and over, King often worked from set pieces, he often repeated himself, and he often improvised on common themes. "The Other America" was initially a talk at Stanford University in April 1967, its title phrase clearly a play on Michael Harrington's monumental 1962 book on American poverty.[7] By March of 1968, when King delivered an alternative version to a predominately Black labor audience in New York, the phrase would have been resoundingly consistent with the findings of the Kerner Commission, which famously concluded that the "nation is moving toward two societies, one black, one white—separate and unequal."[8] King's speech to the 1199ers offers but one window to his thinking about poverty, labor, cross-racial political solidarity, and the Poor People's Campaign (which he had announced in December 1967), among other themes. It also reveals a later King curiously ambivalent about violent protest, or at least the destruction of property. But it is the trope of the "other America," delivered in conversation with working people rather than the Stanford crowd, that helps us to grapple most generatively with the methodological question. In the face of deep racial inequality and inequity, in the face of racial worlds that appear all too separate and unequal, how did King, and how do we, orient and sustain the critical imagination?

"I Don't Consider Myself a Stranger . . ."

On several occasions, King engaged the membership of the United Healthcare Workers East, the predominately African American and Puerto Rican local in New York City, which, at one point, King identified as his favorite labor union.

By the time he delivered his remarks on the two Americas, he said that he considered himself a "fellow 1199er."[9] Though King is often recognized for his later solidarity with the labor movement, in particular his fateful work with the Memphis sanitation workers, it is important, as Lewis Baldwin reminds us, to guard against any notion that King was initially, if not always fundamentally, "some child of privilege who had absorbed uncritically the middle-class ethos and values."[10]

King was of course born into a prominent church family in Atlanta's relatively prosperous Sweet Auburn community, but he was also a born critic whose natural skepticism of both church doctrine and bourgeois society was informed by an unyielding alliance with what Houston Baker has called the "working-class black majority." Foremost in King's critical consciousness, Baker argues, were always "those populations of African, African American, Negro and colored descent in the United States who inhabit the most wretched states, spaces, and places of our national geography," those "black men, women, and children who have little hope for bettering their life chances through any simply (perhaps even 'plausibly') available means." This Black majority, this most "inevitably exposed, severely policed, desperately under-resourced contingent of the African-American population," has become, some fifty years after King's death, "indubitably *the* majority of Afro-America."[11] In order to see King as a critic of racial capitalism and, ultimately, a theorist of an indigenous Black radicalism, we must work from the premise that King was in fact no stranger to Black workers, the Black poor—indeed the Black majority—in the United States and worldwide.

It is also important to acknowledge that King would not have considered himself a "thought leader" as that term is popularly invoked today. King never allowed his thinking to be narrowed or subdued by the parameters of investment worthiness. He was very explicitly an early critic of the conditions that have made the neoliberal "ideas industry" possible, including the empowerment of a plutocratic elite that is able—nowadays increasingly surreptitiously, through seemingly innocuous TED Talks and the like—to commission its intellectual spokespersons and more or less segregate itself from oppositional perspective.[12] Part of what endears us to the King legacy is that his more "comprehensive, activist public intellectualism" stands in such stark contrast to the model of today's neoliberal "thought leader."[13] And while some who set out to challenge the neoliberal paradigm today might question the import of any public intellectualism, comprehensive or otherwise—"we need to drive people to do the hard work needed to take control of the reins of power," insists Lester Spence, and "perhaps we'd do ourselves a service by leaving prophets, even ones like King, and public intellectuals in the past"—we are not convinced that the problems we face today are so glaringly obvious, that the hard work of critical inquiry can be so callously forsaken, or that the "reins of power" as we know them are worthy of immediate pursuit.[14] King insisted, in 1954, that we "must forever stand in judgment upon every economic system."[15] More than a half century on, we simply cannot afford to leave in the past the model of a public intellectualism that is genuinely aligned with the Black majority and that is concerned to build up a Black public that stands in collective judgment.

At a time when public thinking and criticism have become almost entirely circumscribed by plutocratic private interests, we find inspiration in an alternative model of "leadership [that] simply cannot be understood apart from the notion of a black public," or what we might identify, again following Baker, as the "life and institutions of the black majority."[16] How should we understand the nature of this Black public sphere, this discursive space of collective reflection and judgment? What did this public sphere mean for King, in both actual and aspirational terms, and what does and can it mean for us? The very history of Black public intellectualism underscores what is at stake in these questions. In his famous polemic against "spokespersons for the race," Adolph Reed argued that the kind of acquiescent Black public intellectualism favored by the white establishment, the model represented most keenly in the figure of Booker T. Washington, "was a pathological effect of the disfranchisement specific to the segregation era," a result of "black Americans' expulsion from civic life." The absence of a more "vibrant discursive community," Reed said, was only reinforced by the anointing of such spokespersons for the race, and was certainly "a condition to which Washington contributed."[17] By comparison, the contemporary model of neoliberal "thought leadership," circumscribed as it is by market principles and neoliberal rationality—or, as we will suggest, by the terms of racial capitalism—appears to represent a throwback of sorts, a return to a kind of intellectualism that both conditions and is conditioned by the evacuation of public life, including, perhaps especially, a Black radical opposition and the "vibrant discursive community" that such opposition both requires and sustains.

"A Great Deal of Tension . . ."

Built into King's alternative model, giving shape to a public intellectualism that does not consider itself a stranger to the Black masses, is a distinctive methodological and theoretical apparatus, the exposition of which is the focus of the remainder of this chapter. And much of this exposition turns on consideration of King's status as a dialectical thinker. During his graduate student days at Boston University in the early 1950s, King led a Black student reading group known as the "Dialectical Society."[18] A few years later, at the height of the Montgomery bus boycott, he famously identified Hegel, the preeminent modern theorist of the dialectic, as his favorite philosopher.[19] In public statements, and implicitly in many of his most significant writings, King touted his appreciation of dialectical logic and inquiry. We situate King at least partly within the context of what we call the modern dialectical tradition, which, in our analysis, and despite its European lineage, remains a valuable tool with which to expose and critique racial capitalism's social relations. But, as with his critique of racial capitalism, King's indebtedness to this dialectical tradition has to be read into his life and work. For his part, King tended to focus only on tension and synthesis, apparently for him *the* core features of dialectical logic and inquiry.

The first of these, the emphasis on tension, or what we might describe initially as fraught relations between parts within larger totalities, is fundamental for King. Creative tension, what he sometimes referred to in a more political idiom as "creative struggle," was said to drive movement, becoming, and psychic and material growth. The most prominent expression of this sentiment in King's corpus is, of course, the 1963 "Letter from Birmingham City Jail," in which King declared that he was not afraid of a little tension, whether between thoughts in one's mind or between factions within the larger society. Such tension, he seemed to suggest, was precisely the point.[20] This initial emphasis on tension gives way to another idea, likewise central to the modern dialectical tradition, namely, that relations between parts within larger totalities, and the movements born of such relations, are circumscribed by an overarching commitment to rational synthesis.

In 1957, King wrote that Hegel's "analysis of the dialectical process . . . helped me to see that growth comes through struggle." He also stated, without explanation, that Hegel's "contention that 'truth is the whole' led me to a philosophical method of rational coherence."[21] Or, as he put it in 1963, "the philosopher Hegel said that truth is found neither in thesis nor the antithesis, but in an emergent synthesis which reconciles the two."[22] For the most part, King played fast and loose with this idea of dialectical synthesis, or this notion that what it means to think dialectically is to orient oneself toward the reconciliation of generative tensions. Notably curious here, for our purposes, is King's public treatment of Marx, whom we might identify alongside Hegel as the *other* preeminent theorist of the modern dialectical tradition, but whom King fashions, at least in his published writings, as an exponent of "partial truths," an almost undialectical defender of mere antitheses to traditional capitalism, liberalism, and religion, a figure whose positions themselves stand in search of higher synthesis.[23] King's treatment of Marx was often roughshod, if not disingenuous—a fact owed partly to the pressures put upon him by the Cold War context of the 1950s and early '60s. But certainly King was keen to identify tensions—or, in the more technical philosophical language, *contradictions*—precisely because he was convinced that such tensions would be, and indeed should be, moved to reconciliation. At issue, as King aptly describes, is a "philosophical method" built on the presumption of "rational coherence." This presumption is key. When we set out to apprehend lived reality by the lights of a dialectical mode of thinking, the tensions that we experience over time are to be "sharpened," as Hegel used to say, into contradictions and brought to our consciousness as such. And contradictions are said to provoke movement—growth, struggle, our active contestation of the values and norms of lived reality—precisely because, or rather if and only if, contradictions are held to be irrational, and therefore unappealing and unsustainable. It is this overarching rationalism, this commitment to and application of the principle of noncontradiction, that orients the dialectical thinker critically toward the tensions that she experiences and that compels her to put in the hard work necessary to overcome them.

King did not always foreground the moment of rational *synthesis*, and this fact had significant political consequences. In a philosophically rich essay on King and the tradition of dialectical theory, Stephen Ferguson has argued that ultimately King should not be read as a practitioner of a closed Hegelian dialectic. Ferguson argues that King's thinking was affected significantly by the civil rights movement, and by about 1965, "King's dialectics [had] become a dialectic of negation rather than synthesis."[24] Ferguson argues that King grew less interested in trying to reconcile opposing perspectives within the framework of a liberal democratic public sphere, and increasingly concerned to build up a sort of Black radical counterpublic, an oppositional movement that, as "an enemy to capitalism," sought after a "reconstruction of the entire society, a revolution of values."[25] This counterpublic movement is integral to the critique of racial capitalism, and it is important to see that an emphasis on dialectical negation is not an abandonment of synthesis. It is rather the indelible mark of a dialectical critical theorist, one for whom suspicion and skepticism, negative judgment of the reconciliatory prospects of the extant world order, are conditioned and borne along by a driving faith in a reconciliatory world to come, what we might characterize simply as the speculative beyond. As C. L. R. James, perhaps the

preeminent theorist of the dialectic in the twentieth-century Black radical tradition, once said, "it is the unbearable nature of contradiction that creates negativity," for "if there is no sharp contradiction, there is no movement to speak
of, and there is stagnation."[26] In the moment of negativity, in the moment of
critical judgment, the higher rational synthesis may appear impossibly distant.
But for the dialectical thinker it is always there, marking the *unbearable* nature
of contradiction.[27]

James's work on the Black radical import of dialectical thinking is indeed
a fitting comparison. In his midcentury *Notes on Dialectics*, James invoked
Hegel at least in part to highlight the experience of frustration, by which he
meant specifically the sense that our lived experience is often at odds with how
we think or are encouraged to think about ourselves and our situation in the
world. James suggested that dialectical logic can be applied, not as a coping
mechanism, but rather as a sort of cognitive tool with which to sharpen critical
consciousness. A dialectical mode of thinking could be an intentional way to
elevate our experience of frustration consciously to the level of a more pointed
contradiction, which can then be judged and made to motivate political action
aimed at challenging and relieving that frustration—or, as it were, resolving that
contradiction.[28] While King and James knew and admired one another, there is
no indication that King read James seriously beyond perhaps *The Black Jacobins*,
James's seminal history of the Haitian Revolution.[29] But certainly King spoke of
a sense of frustration as if it were an existential affliction endemic to the modern
experience, and a condition that could be actively challenged with the aid of a
little dialectical sharpening. "I've been all over and people are frustrated," King
said, for example, in his speech to the 1199ers. "They're confused, they're bewil-
dered, and they've said that they want a way out of their dilemma. They are angry
and many are on the verge, on the brink of despair."[30] Or, as he put it earlier in
the same speech, "I need not remind you that poverty, the gaps in our society,
the gulfs between inordinate superfluous wealth and abject deadening poverty
have brought about a great deal of despair, a great deal of tension, a great deal
of bitterness."[31] This earlier iteration is especially telling. It would seem that for
King the way out of this mess, the way to challenge this experience of frustration and bitterness, is not merely through its exposure or the simple revelation
of "the other America." We need not be merely reminded, he said. We must
also, as it were, place "the two Americas" into dialectical tension, as contradic-
tory elements that should and must not be allowed to coexist. At issue, in other
words, is the sharpening of our critical consciousness, an exercise that requires a
distinctive set of methodological and theoretical tools.

"The Arc of the Moral Universe Is Long..."

There is more to this methodological and theoretical toolkit. In his account of the political struggles that gave movement to the Montgomery story, King described the activist Rosa Parks in world-historical terms. Parks was "anchored to that seat by the accumulated indignities of days gone by and the boundless aspirations of generations yet unborn," King said. "She was a victim of both the forces of history and the forces of destiny. She had been tracked down by the *Zeitgeist*—the spirit of the time."[32] One must be careful in reading dialectical narratives into human history. There is always a danger, consistent with the legacies of European cultural imperialism, that the preemptory application of a sort of reconciliatory plot structure reduces individual human lives to mere roles in a predetermined drama.[33] This, of course, has been the basis of a common criticism of the Marxist tradition—as King himself, perhaps not coincidentally, pointed out—and it thus presents a danger to secular theorists no less than it does to theistic ones. Given the gravity of this concern, and given King's commitment to both dialectical philosophy and Christian theism, it will be helpful to consider further what Fredric Jameson has called the "diachronic" site of dialectical thinking and criticism, or that which "has to do with telos, narrative, and history."[34]

Consider King's oft-repeated claim, which appears quite prominently in his 1968 speech to the 1199ers, that "the arc of the moral universe is long, but it bends toward justice." If we come at this in abstract moral terms, in the language of good and evil, we might conclude that there is nothing especially dialectical about King's conception of telos, narrative, and history. Good versus evil, while taken by King to reflect a kind of thesis and antithesis embedded in historical process, gives way ultimately to a simple victory of one over the other, the triumph of good over evil. And to be sure, King frequently spoke in these terms. For King, as Rufus Burrow puts it, "no matter how much injustice exists in the world; no matter how badly one group is treated by another, there is a benevolent power that is the beating heart of the universe, one which sides with good, justice, and righteousness."[35] But if we dig a bit more deeply, down to the lived realities and embodied struggles of participants in the historical narrative, then we begin to see that something like a dialectical struggle for reconciliation can be said to actively inform the movement toward what King called the "beloved community."

"The beloved community ideal for King," Lewis Baldwin says, speaks to the "means by which human beings are reconciled to each other and restored to fellowship with God."[36] "The essential end King has in mind," says Vincent Lloyd, "is a world where humans are treated in a way that accords with their infinite value." Lloyd goes on to stress that King is quite clear on the "communal nature" of this beloved community. What King had in mind was not some liberal utopia wherein atomistic individuals voluntarily engage or contract with one another. "Individuals are formed through our relations with each other even if we exceed these relations," Lloyd points out, "and a rich network of such relations must be part of any account of the world we are to desire. It involves not only *absence of contradiction* but also *presence of coherence.*"[37] This telos or end really is a kind of speculative ideal that, to say it again, has the distinctive effect of training critical scrutiny on the ways in which historical human beings are and are not made to be reconciled with each other, in and through their historically embedded social relations. The very structure of this dialectical narrative, of King's effort to apprehend and make sense of lived reality through the application of a reconciliatory mode of narrative emplotment, might be said to *prefigure* an orientation toward the social relations that comprise what we are calling racial capitalism.

This notion of the beloved community underscores, yet again—this time in theistic terms—the enduring value of King's legacy as a critical theorist of negation. As Lloyd has argued, King developed a sort of "negative theology" of the beloved community. While he was "comfortable saying specifically what love is not; we can point to examples of these in the world, the love he commends is ultimately missing, indescribable in worldly terms except in its effects." As such, Lloyd says, "perhaps King does not want us to envision what a beloved community would look like at all. Perhaps that phrase is simply rhetoric that encourages us to interrogate worldly laws that deface the infinite worth of the human being and struggle together to change them."[38] Lloyd's reading captures what we have described as the speculative dimension of the reconciliatory narrative—and, we might note, it does so in quite Hegelian terms, as if the owl of Minerva does indeed take flight only at dusk, only as the Absolute begins to manifest itself in our consciousness, our lived reality. But this reading is also telling because it points toward the possibility that the very narrative structure that King employs, the mode of historical emplotment engendered by his "philosophical method of rational coherence," is intended not necessarily as a human application of God's truth, but perhaps, or perhaps also, as a sort of *rhetorical* tool, part of a methodological and theoretical apparatus that is meant to help historically situated actors take a stand in negative judgment of the world as they experience it.

"And What Is It That America's Failed to Hear?"

When he spoke of tension in the "Letter from Birmingham City Jail," King said that he was concerned "merely [to] bring to the surface the hidden tension that is already alive" in American society. "Like a boil that can never be cured so long as it is covered up but must be opened with all its pus-flowing ugliness to the natural medicines of air and light, injustice must likewise be exposed, with all of the tension its exposing creates, to the light of human conscience and the air of national opinion before it can be cured."[39] King's program of exposing America's underside, of bringing to light what had not been adequately seen or heard, is typically, and rightly, understood as a consciousness-raising enterprise, essentially a program of ideology critique. It is telling that in his speeches and writings, and indeed throughout the secondary literature, enlightenment metaphors abound. King often set out to identify false claims, to right perception, to disclose a more adequate body of knowledge, indeed a more adequate way of knowing. Scholars rightly point out that, "King fought to bring the immiseration of black folks into the light."[40] They have argued that he was "suspicious of the wisdom of the world," and that he set out to show "that the world is not what it seems," indeed that "the wisdom of the world is a mystification used by the powerful and the wealthy to secure their own interests."[41]

By ideology, we refer to a phenomenon in which ideas or values or commitments have become widely held and widely or even universally appealing within a given society, but in such a way that obscures the particular political interests that have fought historically to establish such ideas and that can be said to benefit from their sustained currency. Useful here is Marx's memorable formulation that the "the ideas of the ruling class are in every epoch the ruling ideas, i.e., the class which is the ruling *material* force of society is at the same time its ruling *intellectual* force."[42] The point is just that some people, some group or part of the larger society, can be said to benefit materially from the implementation and maintenance of a particular set of ideas or values. But consider also Raymond Geuss's formulation, which is perhaps more helpful for our efforts to expose a broader sort of ideology critique in King's work. "The existence of specific power relations in society will produce an appearance of a particular kind," Geuss says. "Certain features of the society that are merely local and contingent, and maintained in existence only by the continual exercise of power, will come to seem as if they were universal, necessary, invariant, or natural features of all forms of human social life, or as if they arose spontaneously and uncoercedly by free human action."[43] The critic of ideology, broadly understood, is thus one who sets out to unsettle or problematize widely held ideas and values and commitments, one who sets out to expose the ways in which such ideas and values and commitments have been implemented historically, and in ways that benefit some more than others, or even some at the expense of others.

Consider as an example, and one that speaks quite directly to his broader thinking about political economy, King's critique of the "bootstrapping" ideology that has been, and continues to be, so central to the tradition of American liberalism. This set piece figures prominently in his speech to the 1199ers. The idea is that any one of us can make it in American society, this apparent land of opportunity, if only we put in some hard work. "It is a cruel jest," King countered, "to say to a bootless man that he should lift himself up by his own bootstraps. It is even worse to tell a man to lift himself up by his own bootstraps when somebody is standing on his foot." For Black people in the United States, for the "only ethnic group that has been a slave on American soil," for a people whose idea of self has been stigmatized, whose "blackness" has been rendered synonymous with "something evil and degrading—smut, dirt," for whom "linguistics, semantics [has] conspired against" a requisite sense of dignity and self-confidence, this bootstrapping nonsense is a cruel joke indeed. This joke is only worsened by the underlying historical reality that "nobody . . . in this country has lifted themselves up by their bootstraps."[44] White people have been, and continue to be, disproportionate beneficiaries of practices and policies that have yielded what we might call unearned income and status, from the great material fortunes built on the backs of African slave labor to what David Roediger has referred to, following Du Bois, as the "psychological wages of whiteness."[45]

Typically the critique of ideology is taken to be an epistemic exercise, an effort to debunk illusory perceptions of reality. "The distortions of the world are so great," Lloyd says, "that righting perception is an enormous task." Indeed it is, and certainly this epistemic aspect of ideology critique is an enormous, and enormously important, aspect of King's legacy as a social critic. But one upshot of foregrounding King's dialectical mode of analysis is that it helps to vivify another aspect of King's critical theory, a dimension that in itself is somewhat hidden in his work, and is most definitely missing from the secondary literature, but that is perhaps more befitting of the material challenges wrought by a racial capitalist order. King's dialectical emphasis on tension trains focus on social relations that are hidden or secreted away, not only by the "wisdom of the world," not only by the false or distorted claims of ideological consciousness, but also by the very nature of commercial society. It is in this sense that, in addition to his efforts to cut through false-consciousness and right perception, King can be said to counsel something like the critique of fetishism.

Here we need to lean more heavily on Marx. By itself, fetishism denotes simply the "worship of an inanimate object for its supposed magical powers."[46] But in the tradition of modern critical theory, the fetishism concept is typically invoked as part of an effort to explain the power of commercial society to obscure the complex human relationships that sustain it. Marx said famously that in a market system "a definite social relation between men" assumes "the fantastic form of a relation between things." He was concerned to show that, under conditions of market exchange, our human capacity to engage with one another is almost always mediated by what he called the "commodity-form," or what we might describe as the need to coordinate our human behaviors and preferences exclusively through the exchange of money and according only to the information available to us through price signals. In a commercial society, what appears before us is largely "a world of commodities," a world marked by "material relations between persons and social relations between things." And though Marx referred here to the way the world "appears" to our consciousness, he stressed—and this is really the essence of the critique of fetishism—that the distinctive social relations we experience *appear as what they are*.[47] That our human relationships are mediated by commercial society is no mere illusion. Our failure to see, to respect, and to make decisions based upon genuinely human interactions is not "a made-up construction that can be dismantled if only we care to try."[48] In a consolidated market society, our failure to treat other people as human beings is less a failure than a structured impossibility. What Marx called the "fetishism of the world of commodities" thus reflects our apprehension of a condition that is all very real and true, and that exerts a tremendous hold over each and every one of us.

It is in this sense that, as William Clare Roberts puts it, "fetishism ought to be understood as a form of domination, rather than a form of false-consciousness." We are dealing here with "a political problem first and foremost, and an epistemic problem only derivatively."[49] The exposure of fetishism, then, turns out to be a slightly different operation than the sort of ideology critique that commentators tend to read into King. And yet surely this concern about fetishism, about what becomes of social relations under conditions of market exchange, is strikingly consistent with King's insistence that we need to initiate a "shift from a 'thing'-oriented society to a 'person'-oriented society."[50] This insistence is fundamental to King's critique of capitalist society. The point we wish to make here, in this discussion of methodology, is that the former, the "'thing'-oriented society," is the very reality that we confront. It is ontology as well as epistemology.[51]

And to identify it as such, to cultivate a critical theoretical apparatus appropriate to the analysis of racial capitalism's form of domination, is also to prefigure a distinctive sense of the requisite political work in front of us.

"Too often," Lloyd says, "ideology critique is detached from the complexities of social movement organizing, to the detriment of both."[52] King's legacy, he says, provides an important corrective here. But it is important to emphasize, in ways that Lloyd and other readers of King do not, that capitalism itself, a consolidated market society, is a massively powerful and self-sustaining social movement, a system that reproduces itself through the circulation of commodities. As market actors, we necessarily participate in this movement. As Marx put it, "[our] own social movement has for [us] the form of a movement of things, and instead of controlling it, [we] are under its control."[53] Where readers of King's economic views often point out that he was concerned that "mass production and consumerism dominate society," that "people are focused on buying goods and acquiring wealth in order to buy even more goods," that "our employers, government, and social institutions treat us as numbers, as objects interchangeable with other objects," his readers also tend to conclude that what this means for King is simply that the "world has ... forgotten its soul," that "in a world where people are objects, morality is forgotten."[54] But what we need to see here—and the emphasis on commodity fetishism helps, as does the fuller theoretical account of racial capitalism—is that the task in front of us is not merely to remember morality, not merely to will ourselves to treat human beings as human beings rather than things. In order even to put ourselves in a position to cultivate this sort of collective memory and will, we first need a wholesale transformation of the social form of domination, what King clearly recognized as the "restructuring [of] the whole of American society."[55]

When social relations are mediated by market exchange, Roberts says, we "find ourselves trapped in a giant collective-action-problem-generating machine."[56] It "is not that individuals cannot do exactly what they each want to do, but that they cannot get together and talk about what sorts of things should and should not be done, and what sorts of reasons should and should not count as good reasons."[57] The deliberative space of the democratic public sphere is hamstrung by the fact that we are compelled to reduce ourselves and others to things, to commodities measured by exchange value, and by the fact that we cannot really communicate or learn anything about one another outside of this reductionist apparatus of exchange. This problem is all the more consequential for the cultivation of Black radical counterpublics, for the struggle, King's struggle, to cultivate the desires and wishes of "Negro brothers smothering in an airtight cage of poverty in the midst of an affluent society."[58] We often perceive King as a methodological idealist and a moralist, one for whom the "economic problem" can be remedied with a dose of good, old-fashioned moral willpower. "When it comes to the needs of the 'least of these,'" Lewis Baldwin says in a typical reading of King, "the deficit existed not in human and material resources, but in the human will."[59] But we are beginning to see that weakness of will, what the philosophers call akrasia, is affected greatly by the consolidation of the form of racial capitalist social relations. And we are beginning to see that there is a materialist streak to King's critical theoretical apparatus.

This materialist streak has the effect of sobering the critical imagination. "We have a task," King said, "and let us go out with a divine dissatisfaction." The phrase "let us be dissatisfied," a distinctive cry that King leveled time and again, is perhaps more telling than we know. It would seem to imply that our active discontent with the world is somehow constrained, that something threatens to foreclose even our capacity to challenge the workings of a world in which morality has been forgotten. If, to paraphrase King's Ghanaian comrade Kwame Nkrumah, practice without theory is empty, then perhaps we need to do some theoretical groundwork before we can enjoy the freedom to cultivate and express our discontent.[60] Or, to put it another way, if we share Michael Dawson's interest in rebuilding the Black counterpublic, "quickly and from the bottom up," as King surely did, then perhaps we must set out, as we argue that King did indeed, to expose the "social processes going on behind the backs" of market actors, for "what goes on behind [our] back cannot be contested."[61]

"We Will Bring into Being That Day . . ."

King gestured toward a model of social criticism that was both negative and generative. It was concerned, as Cedric Robinson might put it, with both the "renunciation of actual being" and the disclosure of a "whole other way of being." As we build upon the observations set forth in this chapter and work from an exposition of King's methodological apparatus to reconstruct a critique of racial capitalism, we consider the extent to which King can be understood to exhibit, or at least to work in dialogue with, what Robinson has called the Black radical tradition. Erica Edwards, one of Robinson's most thoughtful contemporary readers, has argued that Robinson set out to "carefully excavate the mechanisms of power," to "detail the radical epistemologies and ontologies that those mechanisms have been erected to restrain," to explore the "ways that people of color, particularly those with African ancestry, pose an imminent threat . . . *and* generate alternative worldviews and ways of being."[62] The Black radical tradition, she says, "is not simply the dialectical antithesis of capitalism or the blind spot of those movements that have posed a challenge to capitalism, such as Marxism," but is, also, "the 'living and breathing' entity that stands 'in the place blinded from view.'"[63] To pursue this "whole other way of being" is to make a decisive break with the very concept of the political, with presumptions and notions of leadership and authority that have been central to this essentially and distinctively Western paradigm. If this is a crucial part of what the Black radical tradition entails, then to what extent can we draw a comparison with King's model of *leadership*, with his struggles to rebuild a Black *counterpublic*, with his efforts to court dissatisfaction and discontent and to "bring into being that day when justice will roll down like waters and righteousness like a mighty stream?"[64] Was King really such a Black radical? And does it really matter? What is at stake?

In the moment of negation, certainly, King was a decidedly political thinker. What we mean by this is that in his effort to uncover and empower "the other America," in his effort to expose the living and breathing human beings most dominated by the social movement of commercial society, King did indeed "pose an imminent threat" to the established order. King's vision of that "whole other way of being," his vision of that "day when justice will roll down," indeed his speculative gesture toward the "beloved community," may well signal, all told, something like the movement toward a postpolitical mode of being. "Justice between man and man [is] one of the divine foundations of society," he said, and he described this not as a *political* ideal but very explicitly as a "high *ethical* notion," the "root of all true *religion*."[65] The implication is that to reflect on ethical relations within capitalist society, or indeed within the "actual being" of racial capitalist modernity, is to foreclose the very possibility of realizing such a "high ethical notion," simply because capitalist relations between things stand in the way of just and ethical relations between human beings. It has been said that "ethics is usually dead politics: the hand of a victor in some past conflict reaching out to try to extend its grip to the present and the future."[66] King had no interest in letting politics die out. It was not yet time. The victor in the past conflict, extending its grip on the present and gravely threatening the future, still had to be reckoned with.

CHAPTER THREE

"Something Is Wrong with Capitalism"

On the Revolution of Values

> [We] built a cotton economy for three hundred years as slaves on which the nation grew powerful. . . . We, too, realize that when human values are subordinated to blind economic forces, human beings can become human scrap.
>
> —Martin Luther King Jr.,
> Speech to the United Automobile Workers

> Something is wrong with capitalism. . . . We are not interested in being integrated into *this* value structure.
>
> —Martin Luther King Jr.,
> Speech to the SCLC National Advisory Committee

"I AM CONVINCED," King said in 1967, "that if we are to get on the right side of the world revolution, we as a nation must undergo a radical revolution of values."[1] This is one of the more resounding lines from King's corpus, and one of the most frequently cited. It is often taken to capture much of the essence of King's later radicalism, a sense of the political commitment and moral urgency that he ascribed to a "second" and more "substantive" phase of his life's work.[2] That second phase sought to organize a more penetrating and comprehensive assault on the "evil triplets": the racism, violence, and cycles of impoverishment that, like a kind of organic compound, had conspired together to give life force to the only American society the world had yet known. It is no secret that King became increasingly outspoken in his dissatisfaction with capitalism and the ways in which racism and violence had been interwoven into the structural workings of the economy and polity of the United States.[3] But we still

33

need a better understanding of the nature, and legacy, of his mature critique of political economy. How, we might ask, is King's call for a "revolution of values" affected by the production and circulation of value in capitalist society?

Though King's analysis moved beyond, often against, key assumptions and conceptual tools of Marxist thought, Marx's way of thinking about capital as "value in motion" is integral to the theory of racial capitalism as we employ it here.[4] Consider again Marx's account of the "commodity-form" under capitalism and how the market actor's singular and largely compulsory focus on the exchange of money can be said to "conceal a social relation."[5] Marx argued that the coordination of human labor and activity, the kinds of human interdependencies that King catalogued under the rubric of an "inescapable network of mutuality," had become sustained in the modern period by a logic of capital accumulation, by a distinctive pressure put upon capitalists—and into the neoliberal moment, essentially *all* market actors—to pursue not only profit, but also sustained growth through the creation of viable outlets for reinvestment.[6] What we are compelled to value and devalue in capitalist society is largely dependent upon its movement through cycles of accumulation and absorption. This movement, this "value in motion," is itself dependent upon the reproduction of social inequalities, which have significant temporal and spatial dimensions, as well as discernible racial dimensions, as the theory of racial capitalism helps us to see.

At issue, then, is something more than what Marx called the "commodity-form." Following Nancy Fraser, we might distinguish between capitalism's economic "front-story," which foregrounds the self-expansion of value through the exploitation of commoditized wage-labor, and its social and political "back-story," which speaks to the semi-or noncommoditized labors and contributions that enable capital accumulation. Capitalism's structural inequalities are maintained partly through economic exploitation and the class relation, but also partly through social and political projects of racial formation. Such racial projects contribute to status differentials, thereby allowing a population to accept as normal, for example, racial overrepresentation in certain job sectors or income brackets or geographical regions of the world economy. Such projects also underwrite the expropriation of value, what Fraser calls "accumulation by other means." For a "crisis-prone system" such as capitalism, in which the pursuit of profit meets routinely with obstacles and limits, all extractive measures remain on the table. Beyond labor exploitation, "commandeered capacities get incorporated into the value-expanding process that defines capital," and political projects of racial formation are a structural pillar of capitalist societies.[7]

King, for his part, claimed to have read *Capital* by himself over the Christmas holiday in 1949.[8] We have acknowledged his avowal of a dialectical methodology, which in its emphasis on processes and interconnections and the movement of parts within social totalities helps to demystify the social relations sustained by the circulation of capital. By invoking Marx's way of thinking about capital as "value in motion," we attempt to allay the spirit of the Marxist "front-story" analysis that King's economic thinking can be said to parallel or exemplify, while also giving ourselves the latitude to include more of the "back-story," in particular the political projects of racial formation.

Once again, in terms of organizational strategy, we parse out significant phrases from one of King's seminal texts in order to broach and work through key themes. For present purposes, the latter portion of the famous 1967 Riverside Church speech is richly suggestive. The imperative, King said from that Morningside Heights pulpit, is to get on the right side of world revolution and to embrace a radical revolution of values. "We must rapidly begin the shift from a thing-oriented society to a person-oriented society," he said, for "when machines and computers, profit motives and property rights, are considered more important than people, the giant triplets of racism, extreme materialism, and militarism are incapable of being conquered."[9] This chapter continues to tease out implicit theoretical assumptions that undergird King's thinking about capitalism, but moves beyond methodological formalism in order to fill in more of the substance. Crucial here is a fuller accounting of King's humanist commitments, including his ideal of the person and his sense that a spiritual dimension of the human experience must be part of any sustainable confrontation with racial capitalism. Crucial, too, is a more substantive accounting of King's narrative commitments. King saw in capitalist modernity an unprecedented, world-historical expansion of human productive and social capacity. But he also saw a "glaring contradiction" in the irrational and immoral persistence of material poverty and racial segregation, the unacceptable persistence of "the other America" and an underdeveloped Global South. It is precisely in his attentiveness to the substance of this signal contradiction that the contours of a theory of racial capitalism begin to emerge in his work. Through analysis, in the latter part of the chapter, of King's speeches and writings on the concentration of Black poverty in the urban North—what King called the "Chicago problem"—as well as a brief consideration of King's anti-imperialism and the internationalist dimensions of his critical theory, we attempt to sketch a more substantive account of how capitalism reproduces the unequal differentiation of human value, how it does so in racial terms, and how this process complicates the call, King's call, for a revolution of values.

"A Person-Oriented Society . . ."

Paul Heideman and Jonah Birch remind us that, "when people first begin to move in collective action against the injustices that confront them, they almost always do so with ideological tools fashioned from their society's dominant ideology. It is only through the course of struggle itself that people begin to discard this ideology in favor of one they fashion themselves, a process epitomized by Martin Luther King Jr.'s radicalization over the course of the 1960s."[10] When King went to Montgomery in 1954, he found a people in movement against injustice, a people who would set out to challenge racial partition by, in part, jamming a wrench into the profitability of a privately owned city bus line.[11] In the broader context of what historians now refer to as the "long Civil Rights Movement," the economic boycott has presented itself as a tried and true strategy.[12] It was never difficult for those on the underside to sense a connection between the logic of capital accumulation and the management of the apartheid state. But for King, when he first began to move in collective action in the American South in the 1950s, his sense of this connection was clouded by the dominant ideological tendencies of the day, certainly by popular attitudes toward communism and capitalism, Marxism and liberalism. There is no doubt that, as Heideman and Birch indicate, King's radicalization over the course of the 1960s, including his sharpened and amplified critique of capitalism, was shaped by his evolving solidarity with the poor, by, as it were, his involvement in the struggle. But intellectually King was never at ease with the dominant ideological tendencies of midcentury American society. From his early days as a seminarian, he found himself drawn to an anti-capitalist humanism, one that shares affinities with both liberalism and Marxism, but that gestures beyond each, or that gives King an intellectual nimbleness that allows him to explore more creative vistas.

In the words of the Rev. J. Pius Barbour, who taught King at Crozer Theological Seminary in the late 1940s and early 1950s, the young King "thought that the capitalist system was predicated on exploitation and prejudice, poverty, and that we wouldn't solve these problems until we got a new social order."[13] Sylvie Laurent has argued that while "King was influenced by his formal training," books and classes simply "provided him with an intellectual framework and curiosity which only substantiated his earliest sentiments, feeding his encompassing critique of an American 'system' in which the words *exploitation* and *capitalism* became inseparable."[14] Still, the academic influences were significant. For our purposes, it will be helpful to highlight his exposure in Boston in the early 1950s to what he called the "personalistic philosophy."[15] On one hand, King's turn to personalism blunted his then-burgeoning radicalism and undergirded the rights-based liberalism of the "first phase" of his movement work. His personalism had the effect of forestalling his embrace of a holistic structural critique of racial capitalism. Yet, on the other hand, King's emphasis on the person—on the material and spiritual needs of each human being, on broad societal and institutional recognition of the dignity of the human personality—clearly informed his mature critique of racial capitalism, as evidenced by his persistent call, central to his Riverside speech and so many others, for a "shift from a 'thing-oriented' society to a 'person-oriented' society."[16]

This avowedly Christian and decidedly non-Marxist philosophical vernacular gave King, in his words, a "metaphysical and philosophical grounding for the idea of a personal God" and "a metaphysical basis for the dignity and worth of all human personality."[17] Many postwar Christian personalists were convinced that politically "there had to be a real revolution, consisting in the creation of a new humanism, where the bourgeois ideal of 'having' would yield to Christian 'being,' a being in communion with others."[18] Every indication is that King, both early and late, was deeply sympathetic to this political vision, and certainly by the time he came to invoke the language of "alienation" in the 1960s, his focus was trained more squarely on a consumerist—or what he referred to somewhat awkwardly as a "materialist"—culture that was thought to warp the human personality and to devalue the reproduction of the beloved community.[19] But we refer to personalism here as a vernacular, a language, because while *personalism* for King was never a philosophical crutch for a narrow liberal individualism—King would stress, repeatedly, that "an individual has not started living until he can rise above the narrow confines of his individualistic concerns to the broader concerns of all humanity"—the emphasis on the *"person,"* on the need to respect the dignity of the *individual*, lends itself to an antidiscrimination politics, the proximate focus of which is the struggle against a discriminatory rights regime, rather than the structural injustices wrought by practices of capital accumulation.[20]

It is in this way that King's Boston personalism fell in line with his conscription into the movement in Montgomery. The dominant ideological tendency of midcentury American society, a rights-based liberalism, shaped the "first phase" of King's work, which took dead aim at measurable obstacles to individual opportunity. Built into this, clearly, was a challenge to extant regimes of capital accumulation, but such a challenge took the form of the tactical boycott, and was never presented as part of a holistic critique of the logic of private wealth accumulation. It could be argued that the proximate goals of the "first phase"—desegregation of bus lines, chain stores, lunch counters, motels—would, if achieved, have the effect of liberating private wealth accumulation, of greasing the gears of American capitalism by allowing living labor to get to work more easily and consumption dollars to circulate more freely. After Montgomery, the SCLC—girded by Old Left veterans such as Bayard Rustin, Stanley Levison, and Ella Baker—had dreamt of spreading a "boycott wildfire" across the South, but was compelled rather quickly to pivot to voter registration, in part because the anti-discrimination politics of a rights-based liberalism obscured the connections between racial domination and capitalist predation.[21] It was not until the campaigns moved north, to the slums of Chicago, that the constituent interconnections of racial capitalism came into bolder relief in a way that King could more openly acknowledge. The point is just that as King found himself called into movement, in the "first phase" of his work, his vision of a "person-oriented society" found itself conscripted by the dominant ideological tendencies of midcentury American society, by the appeal to market principles of liberty and equal opportunity, rather than to the guaranteed satisfaction of human needs.

"Approaching Spiritual Death . . ."

In the Riverside speech, King harkened back to the founding of the SCLC, an organization that set out to "save the soul of America," and he stressed again his longstanding fear of a humanity devoid of spiritual grounding. The personalist theologian Nikolai Berdyaev, with whom King was familiar, wrote in a 1935 essay on Marxism that without the "spiritual element," there "cannot be talk about the attainment of the totality of life." This spiritual element again found concrete expression in King's personalism, and it adds another layer of complexity to King's developing critique of racial capitalism. Throughout his life, King had to reckon with anticommunist hysteria, including American attitudes toward Marxism, and the spirituality question was central to his maneuvering.[22] The pressure he felt to situate his vision vis-à-vis Marxist thought was yet another way in which King was constrained by dominant midcentury ideology. But King's public disavowal of Marxism underscores not only the difficulties he faced in wresting his thinking from the political-economic conservatism of a rights-based liberalism.[23] It also vivifies the ways in which his mature critique of racial capitalism exceeds the terms of European radicalism and exhibits distinctive features of the Black radical tradition.

Berdyaev, for his part, would go on to claim that the "materialist" tradition of Marxist or communist thought "wants to return to the proletariat the means of production alienated from him, but it does not at all want to return the spiritual element of human nature alienated from him, spiritual life." Berdyaev argued that "man belongs not only to the kingdom of Caesar, but also to the Kingdom of God," and that "man possesses a higher dignity and totality, *a value of life*, if he is a person."[24] While King "believed that Marx had analyzed the economic side of capitalism right," like Berdyaev he worried that, as he said to the SCLC staff in 1966, "Marx didn't see the spiritual undergirdings of reality."[25] There is a temptation to read King's emphasis on the spiritual, along with his concern that "materialism" had mushroomed into one of modern society's great evils, as an expression of an overriding idealism of sorts, a sign that his conceptual and methodological moorings discourage any sustained critique of political economy. It is not clear that King ever really understood materialism in a strict Marxist sense of the term. As his former Morehouse College professor Melvin Watson pointed out to him in a 1953 letter, in an effort to correct his reading of Marx, "Marx's position was that the culture, thoughts, in fact, the whole life of man is conditioned . . . *by the means of production*." This "variety of materialism is very difficult to refute," Watson said. And it is, especially for a Baptist preacher steeped in Christian idealism, "a very disturbing phenomenon."[26] But King's point, like Berdyaev's, was just that a strict methodological materialism does not capture the spiritual dimensions of anti-capitalist protest, nor does it honor the ways in which a more satisfactory or sustainable mode of living would make room for the cultivation of spiritual or other meaning-making human activities. And as King put his "personalistic philosophy" into working relation with the movement, his philosophy began to take on characteristic features of the Black radical tradition.

Part of what makes the Black radical tradition, Robinson says, is "the renunciation of actual being for historical being," or the preservation of "the integral totality of the people themselves," a people whose values and principles and ideals exceed the terms of Western modernity. What emerged from indigenous Black struggle in the modern period was a "revolutionary consciousness that proceeded from the whole historical experience of Black people and not merely from the social formations of capitalist slavery or the relations of production of colonialism."[27] The spiritual occupies a central place here, not as an opiate, not as evidence of a reactionary ideological consciousness, but as part of the psychology of active and sustained resistance. This is evident in various stages of King's activism. He went to Albany to join a people "straightening its back," a people working through the *spiritual renewal* that it needed to initiate and sustain collective resistance. He went to Chicago to foment something similar, a *"spiritual transformation* of the ghetto." He went to Memphis to express his *"spiritual connection* with labor," and he found there an audience moved by how his exemplary determination to fight on, his indefatigable courage, was itself reflective of "a *good spirit.*"[28] The spiritual dimension emerges organically from a people in movement and has a sort of autopoietic function, working to persuade the foot soldiers, King included, to stay the course, to keep on the right side of the world revolution, despite the seductiveness of what Robinson called "actual being"—what we might call the inertial allure of white capitalist modernity and its "materialist" trappings of wealth, status, and "all of the other shallow things."[29]

King's worry at Riverside about an approaching "spiritual death" was none other than a concern about the prospective annihilation of a people and its resistance struggles. And it is important to emphasize that this concern is central to the critique of racial capitalism, which trains focus not only on the exploitation of labor and resources, but also on the ways in which logics of capital accumulation render Black people vulnerable to premature death, both corporeally and spiritually. "Accumulation under capitalism is necessarily exploitation of labor, land, and resources," Jodi Melamed says, but it is also "a system of expropriating violence on collective life itself."[30] At issue is a "technology of antirelationality," the "production of social separateness—the disjoining or deactivating of relations between human beings (and humans and nature)—needed for capitalist exploitation to work."[31] Melamed goes on to cite Ruth Wilson Gilmore's seminal definition of racism as "the state-sanctioned and/or extra-legal production and exploitation of group-differentiated vulnerabilities to premature death, *in distinct yet densely interconnected political geographies.*"[32] It is remarkable how well this theoretical framework applies to King's life and work. King was concerned with how Black people had been partitioned and rendered vulnerable, within what he referred to repeatedly as the "inescapable network of mutuality," and in ways that could both feed capital accumulation and foreclose the development of alternative modes of human relation and valuation. King argued in 1966 that "racism is based on the affirmation that the very being of a people is inferior," and that "the ultimate logic of racism is genocide."[33] This conception of racism, this concern with the systematic annihilation of a people, undergirds King's mature critique of how capitalism works as a system of expropriating violence on collective life itself.

"The Glaring Contrast of Poverty and Wealth . . ."

King moved beyond the terms of European radicalism, but he "believed that Marx had analyzed the economic side of capitalism right." Part of what we take this to mean is that King, ever the dialectician, was generally sympathetic with the grand development narrative, the idea that human history can be understood in terms of an ongoing struggle to expand social and productive capacity and that capitalist modernity reflects both historically unprecedented capaciousness and, contradictorily, the persistence of internal obstacles, what Marx referred to as the "fetters," to further development.[34] "Capitalism carries the seeds of its own destruction," King wrote in 1951. "I am convinced that capitalism has seen its best days in America, and not only in America, but in the entire world. It is a well-known fact that no social institution can survive when it has outlived its usefulness. This, capitalism has done. It has failed to meet the needs of the masses."[35] And King was always fond of the maxim, "from each according to his ability, to each according to his needs," which he seems to have regarded as a speculative ideal of sorts, a fugitive vision of a more publicly oriented political economy, one in which human needs are prioritized, in which labor is rendered socially valuable—or "socially necessary," in Marxist terms—only insofar as it is made to serve human needs. The insinuation, again, is that King was worried about how the ideological superstructure of capitalist modernity—established laws and political ideas, shared principles, indeed shared *values*—prevents further development of productive and social capacity, further development of our very ability to relate to one another in ways that serve human needs, both material and spiritual.[36]

And yet, King went beyond the critique of ideology as that operation is conventionally understood. Beyond the demystification of epistemic commitments, King sought to expose a mode of domination built into the material reproduction of capitalism's social form. This aspect of his critique was put on more vivid display as his thinking developed into the mid-to-late 1960s, and as he sought to work through the "glaring contrast of poverty and wealth." The historian Thomas Jackson has shown that by about 1966, King began to argue against not only "lonely islands of poverty in a vast sea of prosperity," but also against the ways in which white privilege and prosperity were themselves conditioned by racial partitioning and Black underdevelopment, how increased capaciousness for some was bought necessarily at the expense of others.[37] Of course King sought to vivify the irrationality of economic inequality and distributive injustice. "Our nation is now so rich, so productive," he said, "that the continuation of persistent poverty is incendiary because the poor cannot rationalize their deprivation."[38] But more to our point, King argued that, "depressed living conditions for Negroes are a *structural part of the economy*," that "certain industries are based upon the supply of low-wage, under-skilled and immobile nonwhite labor."[39]

This line of thinking came alive for King during his time in Chicago, a period that, as David Garrow has shown, "would hasten the expansion of his own critical perspective on American society."[40] In Chicago, King began to speak more openly about the racial dimensions of systemic economic exploitation. A "total pattern of exploitation" is "crystallized in the slum," he said, and this situation exists simply "because someone profits by its existence." Following James Bevel and others, King spoke of "a system of internal colonialism," a "situation [that] is true only for Negroes."[41] Here we begin to garner clues about the spatial or geographical dimensions of King's critique of racial capitalism. At issue is the way in which white wealth and privilege are maintained through, to quote Gilmore again, "the state-sanctioned and/or extra-legal production and exploitation of group-differentiated vulnerabilities to premature death, in distinct yet densely interconnected political geographies." For King, the spatial concentration of Black poverty engendered vulnerability to premature death, both for individuals and for the group, for what Robinson has referred to as "the integral totality of the people." And the urban slum, what King referred to in this moment as "the Chicago problem," was evidence of what Melamed has described as a "technology for reducing collective life to the relations that sustain neoliberal democratic capitalism," a "dialectic in which forms of humanity are separated (made 'distinct') so that they may be 'interconnected' in terms that feed capital."[42] It is worth quoting Melamed at length on this point:

> Although at first glance, dense interconnections seem antithetical to amputated social relations, it is capitalism's particular feat to accomplish differentiation as dense networks and nodes of social separateness. Processes of differentiation and dominant comparative logics create "certainties" of discreteness, distinctness, and discontinuity—of discrete identities, distinct territorializations and sovereignties, and discontinuities between the political and the economic, the internal and the external, and the valued and the devalued. In the drawing of the line that constitutes discrete entities and distinguishes between the valued and the devalued, people and situations are made incommensurable to one another as a disavowed condition of possibility for world-systems of profit and governance.[43]

In his efforts to come to grips with the "Chicago problem," King emerged as a critic who was deftly attuned to the ways in which Black "antirelationality" was densely interwoven with and made to serve circuits of capital accumulation, often through the production of Black vulnerability. He underscored the point that Black people had been partitioned, isolated, immobilized, stigmatized, in essence *devalued*, and that this was a "structural part of the economy."

Consider Marx's definition of devaluation, which is really quite simple in itself, but is useful for thinking about how the value of Black lives is affected by the social movement of capitalist production and exchange. If we think of capital as "value in motion," then we can think of devaluation as what happens whenever and wherever its motion is disrupted. Whenever and wherever the "process of reproduction is checked," Marx says, both "use-value and exchange-value go to the devil."[44] Devaluation must also be seen as "the underside to overaccumulation."[45] Whenever and wherever accumulated surplus is at pains to find viable outlets for reinvestment or absorption, what ensues is the nonproduction of value, or what we might describe more fittingly, highlighting the artificial or manufactured character of the system itself, as the production of nonvalue. As the rate of profit tends to slow system wide, we are confronted with, as Marx put it, "overproduction, speculation crises and surplus capital alongside surplus population."[46] The result is always devaluation. This simple revelation is profoundly significant for how we might understand King's call for a "revolution of values."

Deindustrialization, offshoring, and other forms of capital flight have decimated Black communities in the United States, most proximately in the urban North and the so-called Rust Belt. And though such decimation came into more widespread public consciousness in the decades after King's death—that is, in the wake of the accumulation crises of the 1970s and during the subsequent neoliberal reforms of the 1980s—King appears to have seen the writing on the wall, as his reflections on the "Chicago problem" and his antiwar arguments indicate.[47] In various ways, King found himself pushing back against efforts to resolve the internal contradictions of capital accumulation, efforts by capitalist actors, working in concert with the state, to invest in various ways overseas, to resume circulatory processes that had slowed on the domestic front by creating overseas markets for the absorption of surplus. Throughout the postwar period, such efforts introduced new modes of racial exploitation. It was a "new jungle," King said to a group of packinghouse workers in 1962, made possible by "the shining glittering face of science," by "automation and the runaway shop."[48] The point to emphasize is that what King referred to as a deadening sense of "nobodiness," a sense of neglect and societal worthlessness that he began to read into the material and psychic life of the Black ghetto of the 1960s, was wrought by devaluation—of labor, of education, of infrastructure, indeed of Black lives as such.[49] This kind of racially marked devaluation, to underscore the driving theoretical point, must be seen as an effect of the spatial flight of the circulation of capital.

Michael Denning has pointed out that, "under capitalism, the only thing worse than being exploited is not being exploited."[50] Today we might well refer to "wageless life," to a new manifestation of "surplus population" that, in the words of the *Endnotes* collective, "need not find itself completely 'outside' capitalist social relations. Capital may not need these workers, but they still need to work. They are thus forced to offer themselves up for the most abject forms of wage slavery in the form of petty production and services—identified with informal and often illegal markets of direct exchange arising alongside failures of capitalist production."[51] Wagelessness presents itself, of course, as a major problem for the reproduction of an economy built on the continuous circulation of consumption dollars. And though King knew that "no matter how dynamically the [capitalist] economy develops and expands it does not eliminate poverty," he argued in 1967 that, "we have come to a point where we must make the nonproducer a consumer or we will find ourselves drowning in a sea of consumer goods." He argued that "we must create full employment or we must create incomes. People must be made consumers by one method or the other."[52] It is tempting to read this emphasis on the expansion of consumption power as a sort of temporal fix to systemic accumulation crises, an approach that might buy a little time for the continued circulation of capital and does nothing to challenge underlying structural contradictions, or indeed the reproduction of racial capitalism's social relations. King was ambivalent on this matter, to be sure. But we wager that in his effort to foment a "revolution of values," in his effort to rethink "this value system," King sought to imagine an economy for which consumption would be driven not by the reproduction of capitalism, not by the reproduction of the unequal and obscured social relations that make accumulation possible, but by the service of human needs. His emphasis on propping up consumption power must be understood in the context of this broader critique.

And indeed this broader critique of the reproduction of capitalism, of an economic structure marked by "value in motion," is evident in King's articulation of a strategy of urban "dislocation," which began to emerge in earnest in the summer of 1967. King knew that capital accumulates by "producing and moving through relations of severe inequality among human groups—capitalists with the means of production/workers without the means of subsistence, creditors/ debtors, conquerors of land made property/the dispossessed and removed."[53]

And he sought to galvanize an active countermovement that could challenge the reproduction of racial capitalism on the people's terms. He began to call on Black activists and their allies "to dislocate the functioning of a city," to, as it were, throw sand into the gears of the circulation of capital.[54] Beyond Chicago, King sought to take a poor people's campaign to Washington, to foment a sort of occupy movement that could, in effect, shut it down. If folks could "just camp . . . and stay," he said, "the city will not function." Such a movement, he imagined, could be "as dramatic, as dislocative, as disruptive, as attention-getting as the riots without destroying life or property."[55] The crucial point is just that King's call for "dislocation," a call born of an evolving attentiveness to the racially marked relations and processes that feed capital accumulation, can be understood as part of a movement to reconstruct how human beings relate to and value one another, a strategy that, we are now beginning to see more clearly, is deeply resonant with the Black radical tradition.

"Profit Motives and Property Rights . . ."

The property question adds another layer of complexity. In some settings, in some of his religious sermons for example, King appeared to hold that private wealth accumulation and its legal protection could be justified insofar as it could be made to serve the public good. Christians might be called to do this through moral self-discipline and voluntary acts of redistributive charity, but if this could not be done on a massive scale, then, King was convinced, the dispossessed had to compel a publicly enforced redistribution, and by nearly any means necessary.[56] In other settings, even on those more heated occasions on which he outwardly lamented that "American industry and business, as part of the broader power structure, is in large part responsible for the economic malady which grips and crushes down people in the ghetto," King still appeared to suggest that capital could be hemmed in by a web of regulatory constraints and made to "set aside profit for the greater good."[57] These kinds of suggestions and insinuations cannot be easily squared with King's gestures toward a more comprehensive structural critique of capitalist production, circulation, and exchange.

The property question invites further reflection on King's political-theoretical commitments, in particular his evolving relationship with midcentury liberal ideology. Consider, first, a 1962 speech at the New York convention of the Retail, Wholesale and Department Store Union (RWDSU). Featured here are typical refrains about the "great gulf between superfluous, inordinate wealth, and abject, deadening poverty," about how "there is something wrong with a situation that will take necessities from the masses and give luxuries to the [ruling] classes." King acknowledged again, as he so frequently did, that "we are all caught in an inescapable network of mutuality," but he suggested that "we can work within the framework of our democracy to make for a better distribution of wealth." Speaking to a labor audience, King never broached the question of how the formal protection of private property rights, and thus the protection of a division between the propertied and the dispossessed, is and has been central to "the framework of our democracy."[58] Later on, as he began to differentiate between the first and second phases of the movement, he worried more openly about how first-phase civil rights gains "didn't cost the nation anything." He worried about how a "progress that has been limited mainly to the Negro middle class" did not cut into the distribution and protection of private wealth and power. To "restructure the architecture of American society," to "really mess with folks," King said to his SCLC staff in 1966, you have got to "take profit out of the slums" and begin "messing with the captains of industry."[59]

Two years later, in 1968, speaking to another labor audience in New York, King again committed to working within the framework of American democracy, adhering to liberal protections and representative government, but it was clear that, in the last year of his life especially, King was not altogether convinced that a reformist approach would or could halt the reproduction of systemic political-economic violence. The political scientist Michael Dawson has described King in this moment as a "disillusioned liberal," a figure who had lost hope in the American creed but who was still unsure of where else to turn ideologically.[60] While King had committed to a "massive movement organizing poor people in this country, to demand their rights at the seat of government in Washington, D.C.," he appeared resigned to the very real possibility that such a movement would not significantly impact policy outcomes. And by way of that very sense of resignation he stressed yet again the importance of a kind of spiritual renewal among the soldiers in struggle. "We, as poor people, going to struggle for justice, can't fail," he said. "If there is no response from the federal government, from the Congress, that's the failure, not those who are struggling for justice."[61] In this moment of profound disillusionment with liberal theory and practice, King had declared, in effect, that liberal government was little more than a "committee for managing the affairs of the bourgeoisie," that a liberal rights-based legal and political superstructure is by its nature biased toward the protection and service of propertied interests.[62]

But it is worth noting that King stressed, for example at an SCLC staff retreat in 1966, that "the earth is the Lord's and the fullness thereof. I don't think it belongs to Mr. Rockefeller. I don't think it belongs to Mr. Ford. I think the earth is the Lord's, and since we didn't make these things by ourselves, we must share them with each other."[63] This sentiment leads into another point on the property question, and perhaps also the profit motive. The drive for profit and the protection of property as the so-called fruits of labor were once thought to reinforce "initiative and responsibility." But, King argued, "We've come a long way in our understanding of human motivation and of the blind operation of our economic system." We now "realize that dislocations in the market operations of our economy and the prevalence of discrimination thrust people into idleness and bind them to constant or frequent unemployment against their will."[64] The long history of white wealth acquisition—including what Marx referred to infamously as the "so-called primitive accumulation," what contemporary theorists of racial capitalism might refer to simply as the ongoing expropriation of the Black world—is a haunting testament to the ideological character of classical liberal ideas about property ownership, as King documented in so many words.

Where the beneficiaries of classical liberal doctrine had sought disingenuously to legitimize the protection of private ownership as a way to honor labor and productivity, King sought a "radical redefinition of work" as well as a new way of thinking about how to value and tax property in support of public finance.[65] In this he sought to inspire a radical unsettling of existing common sense and a wholesale rejection of liberal economic and political practice. We know that King praised the dignity of labor in his efforts to uplift the working class and galvanize a potential ally to the Black freedom struggle, indeed a potential army in the fight for the beloved community. But King never romanticized labor as humankind's essential activity. His call for a comprehensive jobs program, and ultimately for a guaranteed annual income, was part of a broader effort to rethink how work and its public appreciation, how "socially necessary" labor, could be transformed to serve human needs, public use-values.[66] Indeed, in the movement from a "thing-oriented" to a "person-oriented" society, King sought to imagine how public service and personality fulfillment could be measured and rewarded as socially necessary human labor, work that in itself would disrupt the reproduction of capitalism's social form. Imagining how an unemployed man might be put to work and compensated, King said that, "if he had a whole year to do nothing but read sometimes, and then go around meeting people, and shaking hands, and talking with them about their problems, that is work. He ought to be paid to do that."[67] Though it is tempting to read King here as a Proudhonist of sorts—a reformer concerned to manipulate compensation structures without necessarily challenging the systemic reproduction of capitalist social relations—King's economic imaginary portends a whole new mode of human relation, a range of new possibilities that he knew had been discouraged, if not altogether forbidden, by the "actual being" of racial capitalism.

"Our problem," King said repeatedly during his last years, "is that we all too often have socialism for the rich and rugged free enterprise capitalism for the poor."[68] This problem, our problem, has grown worse over time.[69] And today's socialism for the rich is financed primarily through the taxation of labor and production, which has had the effect of suppressing employment and offshoring profit. True to his conviction that "the earth is the Lord's, and since we didn't make these things by ourselves, we must share them with each other," King sought to shift the tax burden toward land ownership and real estate, in an effort to help arrest cycles of unemployment and expropriation. King never furnished a concrete tax proposal, but his overtures toward tax reform, in particular his fondness for the so-called land-value tax, underscore a driving concern that land acquisition had long been one of the central mechanisms through which, to quote Robinson again, racialism came to permeate the "social structures emergent from capitalism."[70] Glaring are the racial disparities in land ownership and the intergenerational wealth reproduced through its institutional protection, and King's point was simply that the dispossessed had to confront legal protections and ideas about ownership and obligation in order to challenge those unequal human relationships through which capital accumulates. As Jesse Myerson and Mychal Denzel Smith note in a recent essay on King's legacy, "no human created the land, and so no one—not an absentee slumlord, not Goldman Sachs—should be extracting its value from the people who live on it."[71] In his challenge to land ownership, what King sought, in this "second phase" of the movement, was nothing other than a struggle to finally make white America pay.

"Social Stability for Our Investments . . ."

Land concerns were also a consistent pillar of King's global vision, as evidenced by, for example, his early interest in the Indian Bhoodan Movement and, of course, his mature defense of the Northern Vietnamese struggles for land reform.[72] By 1967, and to the consternation of so many in and outside of the movement, King offered an apology of sorts for a Northern Vietnamese "revolutionary government seeking self-determination," a "government that had been established not by China—for whom the Vietnamese have no great love—but by clearly indigenous forces that included some communists." For the peasants of the Vietnamese countryside, King said, "this new government meant real land reform, one of the most important needs in their lives."[73] The Riverside speech was a grand culmination of King's vision in so many ways, though many of the themes we have addressed so far in the chapter receive only passing mention. More central to the speech is King's call for a revolution of values within the racial violence of the capitalist world system, though even this is often obscured on account of the dominant ideological framework of American neo-imperialism.

Too often appreciation of King's internationalism is hemmed in by a narrow reading of his opposition to the Vietnam War. A 1967 *New York Times* editorial set the tone for subsequent reception when it framed "Dr. King's error" in terms of a "facile connection between the speeding up of the war in Vietnam and the slowing down of the war on poverty."[74] Such a reading, supported to be sure by King's own insistence that "our government is more concerned about winning an unjust war in Vietnam than winning the war against poverty here at home," reduces the economic dimension of King's antimilitarism to a matter of opportunity costs, as if the only relevant question has to do with domestic budgetary priority, how best to allocate federal expenditure.[75] But at Riverside King was clear that "the need to *maintain social stability for our investments* accounts for the counterrevolutionary action of American forces in Guatemala" and explains why "American helicopters are being used against guerrillas in Cambodia and why American napalm and Green Beret forces have already been active against rebels in Peru." The systemic need for the continuous circulation of capital and the ongoing expansion of its spatial boundaries—the dynamic structural imperative of the global market economy—accounts for "our alliance with the landed gentry of South America" and explains why we see "individual capitalists of the West investing huge sums of money in Asia, Africa, and South America, only to take the profits out with no concern for the social betterment of the countries." King described postwar U.S. imperialism in terms of a stubborn global class politics, an elite refusal "to give up the privileges and the pleasures that come from the immense profits of overseas investments."[76] The implication, on a deeper theoretical plane, is that warfare had become a crucial resource in the capitalist struggle to resolve escalating accumulation crises. What King sought to confront, in essence, was a proactive government movement seeking to establish and maintain overseas markets for the absorption of economic surplus. King's antiwar arguments ought to be seen as part of a long tradition of left criticism of military surplus spending, what he might have described as "military Keynesianism."[77]

The key forebear of that long tradition of left criticism once said that "an industrial army of workmen, under the command of a capitalist, requires, *like a real army*, officers [managers], and sergeants [foremen overlookers], who, while the work is being done, command in the name of the capitalist."[78] For so long, within that left tradition, it was presumed that the "silent compulsion" of market relations would come to supplant more violent dispossession and expropriation of land and labor, that the naked violence that Marx read into capitalism's "prehistory" would over time take on a more covert *modus operandi*. It was presumed that market rationalization would obscure the ways in which "free" living labor would continue to be thrust into impoverishment and expendability, that the work of ideology critique would thus become an increasingly salient weapon in the ongoing class struggle. Fair enough. Ideology critique is crucial work, as we have seen. But it is important to invoke the theory of racial capitalism here, as the privileged vantage of European radicalism has not always registered the real violence, racial and otherwise, that King and other twentieth-century Black radicals have borne prophetic witness to. From the vantage of Black labor and wageless life worldwide, there is and has been nothing *analogous* about the role of military discipline and management in the production and circulation of value. Capital accumulation requires *real armies*, commanding and supervising market relations on a global scale. And in this, racial domination plays an essential role.

Recent historical work has documented the ways in which early capitalism specialized in, as Nikhil Pal Singh puts it, a "form of commercial privateering backed but unimpeded by sovereign power and most fully realized in slavery, settler colonialism, and imperialism."[79] Certainly the "conscription, criminalization, and disposability of poor, idle, or surplus labor—the historical process of forcibly 'divorcing the producers from the means of production' that for Marx is capitalism's precondition," has always relied upon "racial differentiation as a directly violent yet also flexible and fungible mode of ascription." But, as Singh goes on to point out, "there has been no period in which racial domination has not been woven into the management of capitalist society."[80] The "state-sanctioned force and violence originally required to create wage labor" has not disappeared into the era of mature, consolidated global capitalism. Indeed into our own time, force and violence is "retained in the forms of hierarchy and competition between workers, in the social requirements of policing unwaged labor that has migrated to poverty and the informal economy, and in imperial and nationalist interpellations of the urban and metropolitan working classes."[81] King spoke of expanded social and productive capacity under capitalism, population increase and improved living conditions, but he also underscored as the precondition their dialectical underside: the production of human scrap, the disposability of living labor, and the omnipresent threat of systematic annihilation of a people. Here we would do well to recall, to quote Singh again, that the "constant, violent dislocation of these two processes requires constant management in the form of police and military solutions—that is, directly coercive interventions." Capital accumulation "spurs forms of moral, temporal, and spatial sequestration that become part of the framework of crisis management, through which the simultaneous production of growth and death can be viewed less as a contradiction than as a necessary dimension of historical progress."[82] It cannot be denied that in this, racial ascription and domination play an essential role.

These sobering considerations can be read back into King's suspicions of global capitalism in richly generative ways. The imperial expansion of the capitalist value-form has put more and more human beings in relation to one another in ways that feed the production and circulation of capital. As Samir Amin reminds us, "far from progressively 'homogenizing' economic conditions on a planetary scale," this historical process has produced racial inequality and uneven geographical development, a "permanent asymmetry" in which is "affirmed, with violence still greater than that contemplated by Marx, the law of pauperization that is indissolubly linked to the logic of capital accumulation."[83] This is precisely what has become of the "inescapable network of mutuality," what will remain of it, King feared, unless enough conscientious objectors step up to confront—actively and politically, and not merely through the cultivation of moral conscience or right perception—the war-making and imperial offensives that reproduce the conditions for the production and circulation of value worldwide.

It is important to note that King's antiwar arguments were carved against a burgeoning midcentury Black internationalism, at a time when he found himself immersed in what Brandon Terry has called the "problem-space of black power."[84] This was a context in which a "resurgence of Marxist thought in black political life helped enable a shift away from the discourse of *inclusion* and *citizenship rights*, toward emphases on *oppression* and *domination*," but also a context in which Pan-Africanist commitments augured a renewed sense of global anti-capitalist solidarity.[85] King's "second phase" marked his reorientation toward criticism of structures of oppression and domination, and it could be argued that this context enabled his Pan-Africanism in compelling ways, too. As Terry goes on to point out, "King often invoked African Americans' connection to Africa, and suggested modes of transnational solidarity," though "his formulations placed less emphasis on the idiom of 'racial' ancestry than resonant and shared features of racial oppression between colonialism and Jim Crow."[86] And in this way, King's internationalism hewed closer to the spirit of Bandung, the spirit of an anti-capitalist, nonaligned movement born of a global Southern alliance, a resonant and shared experience of racial and colonial oppression. It is telling that for King, the landmark 1955 gathering in Bandung, Indonesia, spearheaded by twenty-nine Asian and African delegations caught in the throes of anti-imperialist struggle, was better understood as a popular movement than a national or bourgeois one. "More than one billion three hundred million of the colored peoples of the world have broken aloose from colonialism and imperialism," King said to a crowd in St. Louis in 1957. "*They* have broken aloose from the Egypt of colonialism.... *They* assembled in Bandung some months ago."[87]

"These Are Revolutionary Times ..."

At Riverside Church a decade later, King spoke again of politics and of where the future might go. He urged solidarity with grassroots struggles of various kinds. "All over the globe men are revolting against old systems of exploitation and oppression," he said, "and out of the wounds of a frail world, new systems of justice and equality are being born. The shirtless and barefoot people of the land are rising up as never before. The people who sat in darkness have seen a great light." It is incumbent upon all of us, he said, to "support these revolutions."[88] Within the U.S. context, King was drawn to a burgeoning Black youth movement that had begun its own revolution of values through indigenous confrontation with "actual being." It was "precisely when young Negroes threw off their middle-class values that they made an historic social contribution," he said.[89] And it is perhaps worth noting that, in the last year of his life especially, King was tempted to move out of his nonviolent comfort zone in an effort to grapple with modes of indigenous protest against the coming of the new phase of the capitalist economy, what critics refer to today as the neoliberal world order.

It is remarkable how well King's mature reflections on political economy transcend their historical genesis. As the historian Thomas Holt has documented, into the 1970s and 1980s, into the accumulation crises of the early neoliberal era, "blacks found themselves the late-arriving guests as the feast for an expanding middle class was ending." In the throes of deindustrialization, as the "post-production" domestic economy came to resemble "a zero-sum game rather than an expanding pie, policies of racial preference became the scapegoat for a tightening labor market and concentration of educational opportunities."[90] Joshua Clover has argued that the riot, rather than the traditional labor strike, is the mode of anti-capitalist protest that follows organically from the lived realities of a "post-production" phase, a moment marked by a glaring coupling of surplus capital and surplus population. Where the industrial labor strike is a "form of collective action that struggles to set the price of labor power, is unified by worker identity, and unfolds in the context of production, *riot* struggles to set prices in the market, is unified by shared dispossession, and unfolds in the context of consumption." The riot, Clover says, "is a circulation struggle because both capital and its dispossessed have been driven to seek reproduction there."[91] It is worth noting that King, in the last year of his life, became far more ambivalent about riotous protest than his sanitized legacy has been made to lead on. Though King never outwardly condoned the riot, he sought to understand and explain riotous protest as an indigenous reaction to circulation crises and the dispossession wrought by the racial-capitalist edifice. Indeed for King, the riot was an indigenous reaction on the part of a "surplus population confronted by the old problem of consumption without direct access to the wage."[92] Whereas the "American economy in the late 19th and early 20th Centuries . . . had room for—even a great need for—unskilled manual labor," whereas once "jobs were available for willing workers," in 1968, King said, "there are fewer and fewer jobs for the culturally and educationally deprived; thus does present-day poverty feed upon itself. The Negro today cannot escape his ghetto."[93] King drew a distinction, consistent with his personalism, between violence against people and violence against property; the latter, he said, is always the object of riotous violence and makes a degree of moral sense insofar as property, the symbol of bourgeois values, is structurally prevented from serving the needs of vulnerable human beings, the needs of living persons.[94] The relevant point, in any case, is that toward the end of his life King appeared to have anticipated the expansion of the racialized surplus population as well as the inevitability of its modes of resistance, the people's "methods of escape."[95]

Today scholars argue that the rapid economic growth of the mid-twentieth century is beginning to look more and more like the great historical exception and that the zero-sum tendencies of the neoliberal era indicate a likelihood that no type or degree of government intervention can do much to build out prosperity or even sustain an existing middle class.[96] But as we discuss more fully in the next chapter, King's arguments for the recovery of a more robust, state-sponsored social welfare contract are not anachronistic, nor are his gestures toward more informal and thus more creative political responses. For many conventional economists, concerns about neoliberal growth crises are circumscribed by an academic commitment to liberal principles, by a desire to protect private sector

freedoms and expand markets, rather than to foment politically driven redistribution.[97] King knew as well as any trained economist that markets coordinate
human preferences, but by the time he called for the mass mobilization of poor
people, he must have concluded that markets simply do not see the poor because
the poor have nothing to offer and cannot be fitted into their mode of valuation.
If the new economy is fraught with accumulation crises and is moving toward
a zero-sum relation between winners and losers, then we ought to expect a new
era of politicization. We ought to expect that future resistance, disillusioned as
was the later King, will set out to work both within and beyond conventional
channels of liberal democracy. The mature King knew all too well that "some
Americans would need to give up privileges and resources for others to live in
decency." And he knew all too well that "that took politics."[98] We turn now to
consider more fully the complicated status of the political in King's critique.

CHAPTER FOUR

"Showdown for Nonviolence"

On Black Radicalism and the Antipolitical

The greatest purveyor of violence in the world today: my own
government.

—Martin Luther King Jr., *The Trumpet of Conscience*

The fact that black men govern states, are building democratic
institutions, sit in world tribunals, and participate in global
decision-making gives every Negro a needed sense of dignity.

—Martin Luther King Jr., "Let My People Go"

K ING LIVED THROUGH AN ERA of state-managed capitalism. He
struggled mightily with the contradictions of that era. An explicit and
consistent champion of the welfare state, King fought for a government
that could enforce capital controls, redistribute wealth and power, and institutionalize a greater measure of democratic accountability. But he knew that the
very model of the welfare state was designed to save capitalism from itself, in part
by propping up a consumerist "materialism" that his moral conscience could not
accept. He knew that the welfare state had been wedded historically to an abiding white supremacism and that any regulatory provisions would always threaten
to build out only a kind of herrenvolk democratization—egalitarian gains for
a white middle class. And as his later anti-imperialist arguments indicate, he
was deeply concerned that the material wealth that made the United States and
other Northern welfare states possible was itself largely a product of the historical and ongoing underdevelopment of the Global South.

Nation, state, government—these political categories factor uneasily into
King's critique of capitalism. A similar uneasiness pervades much of the

55

contemporary criticism. Intellectuals and organizers today often take explicit aim at the very idea of the state, an apparatus of power that has always subjugated and meted out violence against Black lives. And yet pervasive is the call for that same apparatus of power to administer regulations, subsidies, redistributions, and reparations.[1] This raises questions about the status of the political in the critique of racial capitalism, past and present. Cedric Robinson argued that the historical consolidation of capitalist society established a conception of the political rooted in presumptions of authority, leadership, and order. "The political came to fruition," he argued, "with the theory of the State as the primary vehicle for the organization and ordering of the mass society produced by capitalism."[2] This state-centered conception of the political has since been consumed by the loaded question of how we shall be governed, rather than by more open-ended questions of how we want to live or to be. The political, in other words, is inherently repressive. But Robinson's work is meant to show that there was always a limit to the pervasiveness of the state's governing reach. There was always a contingent and mythical character to the paradigm of the political. In the Black radical tradition especially, in the freedom-fighting communities that were often "blinded from view" by Western scholarship and political science, there emerged, or perhaps survived, latent ideas and practices of living and being together that were not so easily circumscribed by the political and its defining presumption of governability.[3]

In this chapter we invoke King's posthumously published essay "Showdown for Nonviolence" to anchor a discussion of King's two conceptions of the political and to situate King, finally, within the Black radical tradition. King's thinking about state-managed capitalism discloses the layered nature of his political theory. In his more conventional mode, he affirms the idea of a democratically accountable welfare state, both domestically in the United States and in ways that anticipate the globally scaled "world welfare" model that emerged most prominently in the 1970s in the postcolonial Global South. But he also underscored how efforts to work within the conventional paradigm, how grassroots struggles to pressure the existing state apparatus to expand public control, to achieve some semblance of a more popular grip over the worst excesses of racial capitalism, also yielded new social sympathies and solidarities that could ground and inform alternative ways of living and being together. At issue is a Black democratic praxis that exceeds racial capitalism's dominion. Much of this is captured in King's speculative grasping after what he called the "beloved community." And though it is tempting to read these aspirational dimensions of King's thinking as a flight into ideal theory, they are better understood, we argue, as a concrete expression of the Black radical tradition.

"We Will Call on the Government . . ."

"Showdown for Nonviolence" begins with reference to state violence. "The policy of the federal government is to play Russian roulette with riots" and to "gamble with another summer of disaster."[4] Written on the cusp of what King feared would be another long, heated season of urban uprisings, the essay sought to rally support for the Poor People's Campaign and to mobilize masses of American residents who would "call on the government" to "correct" the causes of violent rebellion. But undergirding that call, as always, was the insinuation that government policy, the state itself, was directly responsible for the reproduction of human misery, the very conditions that led to popular unrest. As King argued more pointedly two months earlier at a rally in Mississippi, "poor people are victimized by a riotous Congress and welfare bureaucracy," by "the insult of closed housing statutes," by "schools which are institutions of disorder and neglect," by "flame throwers in Vietnam [that] fan the flames in our cities." He stressed that as "the lives, incomes, the wellbeing of poor people everywhere in America are plundered," it is "no wonder that men who see their communities raped by this society sometimes turn to violence."[5]

In "Showdown," King went on to cite the U.S. government's own conclusion that racism was threatening the "destruction of basic democratic values." He referenced the Kerner Commission's plea for "national action—compassionate, massive and sustained, backed by the resources of the most powerful and the richest nation on earth."[6] Again, King's appeal to what he called "national salvation," to a conception of the state as both cause of injustice and instrument of correction, is nothing new to his readers, especially those who regard him as a kind of egalitarian or perfectionist liberal. In this section we highlight two perhaps lesser-known aspects of King's thinking about the very idea of the welfare state, both of which came into bolder relief during the last two years of his life.

The first aspect underscores the extent to which King's views on welfare policies, and indeed the nature of exploitation and expropriation within capitalist society, were expanded and further "radicalized" by welfare rights activists in and after 1966. King, of course, was never alone in voicing his discontent with the limited nature of the Johnson Administration's War on Poverty. At the time, several welfare rights groups coalesced to form the National Welfare Rights Organization (NWRO). Antipoverty organizers such as Johnnie Tillmon, Beulah Sanders, and George Wiley, among many others, sought to challenge prevailing attitudes about work and welfare and to lobby aggressively for more expansive policies, including a federally guaranteed annual income. In 1968, when King sought the endorsement of the NWRO in the run-up to the Poor People's Campaign, Tillmon in particular took him to task for failing to grasp the full extent to which government policies dehumanize the poor, reduce Black women to statistics in a management scheme, and reproduce racism, classism, and patriarchy—what Tillmon referred to as the philosophy of "the man."[7] During a panel discussion at a conference in Chicago, as King fumbled through questions about pending welfare legislation, Tillmon said to King, "You know, Dr. King, if you don't know, you should say you don't know." King admitted that he had an inadequate grasp of the issues at hand and had "come to learn."[8]

The historian Sylvie Laurent has shown that Tillmon and the NWRO articulated and practiced a "radical vision of citizenship," which had a profound impact on King. King knew that "race trumped class in the management of social welfare distribution," and that "antiwelfare policies, particularly those involving the surveillance of recipients, were inscribing criminality onto every aspect of the lives of disinherited African American families."[9] But the NWRO "reframed" debates about work and welfare, "arguing for the 'right to an income' to replace ubiquitous yet prejudiced concepts of worthiness and deservedness." According to Laurent, this helped King see more clearly that "single mothers were entitled to their own income" and that antipoverty activism had to challenge the "patriarchal concept of family wage." The NWRO "awakened [King] to the double blind of poor black women, notably mothers who, insofar as their work was unpaid, were working poor too."[10]

In many ways a "man of his time," King failed miserably to grapple with the full economic significance of gender and patriarchy.[11] He never fully wrested his economic policy prescriptions away from the presumption of a "family wage" for a male breadwinner or from ideas about just compensation for those who "want to work and are able to work."[12] But his eventual call to "guarantee an income to all who are not able to work," and his more expansive and imaginative ideas about "creating certain public service jobs," gesture toward new thinking about how to revalue and compensate all of the expropriated work and labor, disproportionately borne out by Black women, that is needed to sustain a regime of capital accumulation. And to Laurent's point, much of this appears to have been impressed upon King by Johnnie Tillmon and other Black radical welfare rights activists.

King's inquiries into the role that the state can play helped him build out his critical theory of racial capitalism, perhaps even to the point of seeing more clearly capitalism's gendered nature, that other pillar of what Nancy Fraser has called the "back-story" of social reproduction that conditions the possibility of capitalism's "front-story" of commodity production. Included in that backstory, writes Fraser, are "the forms of provisioning, caregiving, and interacting that produce and maintain social bonds," the reproductive labor of mothers, certainly, but also the broader "work of socializing the young, building communities, and producing and reproducing the shared meanings, affective dispositions, and horizons of value that underpin social cooperation." Throughout capitalism's history, this social-reproductive work has been separated from the market, formally unrecognized and uncompensated. Yet, "social reproductive activity is absolutely necessary to the existence of waged work, to the accumulation of surplus value, and to the functioning of capitalism as such. Wage labor could neither exist nor be exploited, after all, in the absence of housework, child-raising, schooling, affective care, and a host of other activities that produce new generations of workers, replenish existing generations, and maintain social bonds and shared understandings."[13] Moreover, the capitalist push to drive down production costs, to exploit efficiencies and offload risks and responsibilities, tends to eat away at social-reproductive capacity, especially among vulnerable populations. Fraser calls this "capitalism's built-in tendency to social-reproductive crisis."[14] And the great *political* movements of the twentieth century—the labor movement, certainly, but perhaps even more significantly women's and Black liberation struggles—emerged as powerful agents of crisis management. These *political* struggles shed light on capitalism's backstory and helped to establish public provision, the welfare state, as means of mitigating and forestalling systemic crisis.

Thus to heed the promise of "national salvation," as King consistently did, to adhere to the notion of an expanded welfare state that could create jobs (even wildly imaginative new "public service" jobs) or otherwise recognize, compensate, and sustain social-reproductive work, is to reinforce state-managed capitalism. But crisis management always has its limits. This is especially true of capitalism's crisis tendencies, as the benefits and protections afforded by state provision were never really extended beyond a relatively privileged few. Racial asymmetries and patriarchal norms, though meaningfully challenged, were never fully overcome. "Although the state-managed regime succeeded in pacifying capitalism's crisis tendencies in the core for several decades," writes Fraser, "it could not definitively master them." From King's era onward, "cracks in the edifice began to appear: the 'productivity crisis,' 'the fiscal crisis of the state,' and a full-scale crisis of legitimation."[15] And state-managed capitalism had to confront its contradictions beyond those felt in the core countries, across the decolonizing and postcolonial Global South. And here we pivot to the second aspect of King's thinking about the welfare state and his "national salvation" approach, namely, its international or transnational implications. This requires a foray into the speculative. Aside from a passing remark in 1964 about the need to "consider some form of world government," King said very little about how the model could be extended beyond the U.S. national context.[16]

In the late 1950s, the sociologist Gunnar Myrdal began to articulate the idea of a globally scaled welfarism, what he called "welfare world."[17] This was a decade or so after the publication of *An American Dilemma*, Myrdal's pioneering study of race relations in the United States, which King cited many times throughout his career. There is no indication that King encountered or engaged with Myrdal's later work on international political economy, but King's analysis of global capitalism and his appeal to state redistribution clearly align with Myrdal's international vision, which coincidentally also parallels the development and internationalist agendas of several prominent postcolonial leaders in the decade immediately following King's death.[18]

Myrdal built his argument not on any moral appeal to human rights, but rather on the socio-historical premise that we have been discussing, namely, that the redistributive politics of the rich countries, and the "national solidarities" that enabled such redistribution, had mitigated systemic crisis and forestalled capitalism's self-destruction. "Marx's prophecy" that capitalism would cannibalize itself may have "been proved wrong for the individual nations," but Myrdal worried at midcentury that it could "turn out to be an accurate forecast in regard to the relations among nations."[19] He saw the global scaling of the welfare model as a necessary next step in forestalling systemic crisis. And of course, this next step posed significant challenges, principally, as Samuel Moyn and others have pointed out, that "*the nationalist policies that had made the welfare state possible at home* now impeded its institutionalization abroad."[20] That is, the twin expansion of state capacity and nationalist sentiment brought domestic working classes under a kind of state protectionism, forged a transactional, if not fiercely competitive, relationship between national populations on the global stage, and effectively disincentivized an international redistributionism. Quite relevant here is King's evolving frustration with organized labor in the United States, which during King's lifetime often reflected both the reactionary racial politics of American nationalism and a strident complicity with a neo-imperial foreign policy that for many union leaders was thought to secure jobs and benefits on the home front.[21]

Still, the scaled welfare challenge was taken up directly by the next generation of postcolonial leaders, most notably Tanzania's Julius Nyerere and Jamaica's

Michael Manley. Adom Getachew points out how Nyerere, in particular, articulated an important reformulation of the theory of sovereign equality. "Just as equal political citizenship within the state does not undo the 'dependence and dominance' of the 'man who needs to sell his labor in order to buy bread,' formal sovereign equality left intact the dependence of postcolonial states." For Nyerere, "the discrepancies between formal equality and substantive inequality had to be rectified if sovereign equality was to be a meaningful principle of the international order."[22] This line of thinking more than echoes King's "second phase" critique of substantive economic inequality, which undergirded his emphasis on domestic welfarism in the United States. It takes very little imagination to stretch King's famous hamburger-at-the-lunch-counter query and to picture King asking, "What does it profit peoples of the Global South to integrate into the international system if they do not have the capacity to compete economically?"[23] Moreover, the world welfarism of the New International Economic Order (NIEO) was seen, again, as an effort to stave off crisis; conceptualizing the Global South as the workers of the world, in a way not unlike King's emphases on global economic interdependence and the "inescapable network of mutuality," the idea was to shore up the global bases of exploitation and expropriation in ways that would provide some relative benefit to the workers of the world and stabilize the capitalist system. "While equitable globalization entailed preferential treatment for postcolonial states, proponents of the NIEO argued that it was in service of the global economy more broadly," an "internationally managed global economy that was structured by equitable interdependence rather than hierarchical dependence."[24]

On a practical level, beyond gestures toward the United Nations General Assembly as the sort of political institution that could facilitate a new egalitarian internationalism, proponents of the NIEO and world welfarism were unable to chart a pragmatic course of action. Myrdal, for example, and perhaps not unlike King on matters of economics, was known to be much stronger as a diagnostic critic than a prescriptive policymaker. Myrdal would argue for the building out of a kind of global public sphere in which the grievances of Global South nations could be articulated and amplified, a Southern "Great Awakening." In the postwar period, he pointed toward, in the words of Moyn, "a broad public not only south but also north accepting rising levels of inequality as an embarrassment."[25] Of course King, for his part, clearly understood that rich countries would not voluntarily redistribute wealth and that in the absence of a hard-fought redistribution of power, such almsgiving would be counterproductive.[26] But like King's calls in "Showdown" and elsewhere to "dramatize" poverty, like Johnnie

Tillmon and other welfare rights activists' struggles to raise consciousness and reframe public debates around race-and gender-based domination, proponents of postcolonial world welfarism saw a need to organize historically oppressed communities, both domestically and globally, such that pressure could be applied to wealth and power. This basic appeal to democratic accountability is the pivot between King's two conceptions of the political.

"A New Kind of Togetherness . . ."

In his more conventional mode, King appears to have thought of the state as an instrument to be used for more or less democratic purposes. In this mode, he worked from a conception of the political that is "dominated by the positivity of the State" and that bears the imprint of the historical consolidation of market capitalism.[27] This conception of the political, Robinson argues, "found convenience with the exigencies of certain sectors of the population of the new, class-conscious society" that emerged with modern capitalism. The "functional interests of these classes fell within the capabilities of the State as an administrative apparatus, thus confirming its significance in utilitarian terms." And all of this had a profound effect on ensuing waves of democratization. As the positivity of the state became more stable and entrenched, democratic aspirants were reduced essentially to "claimants," the struggle for democracy to a question of state capture.[28] Could the working classes, could other expropriated groups or constituencies, effectively bend the administrative apparatus more in their favor? What was rarely, if ever, challenged was the presumption of state authority itself, the presumption that political subjects must and should and indeed will be governed.

We might think of King as a willing conscript in these quintessentially modern struggles for statist accountability. He was a man of his time. But he clearly recognized how democratic aspiration gets circumscribed and, in many ways, reduced by the conception of the political that undergirds the statist model. "I do not think of political power as an end," King said in 1966, "neither do I think of economic power as an end."[29] The call to prepare government programs, he said in 1967, "distracts us excessively from our basic and primary tasks."[30] The objective for King was never to register formal claimants vis-à-vis the racial capitalist state. It was never to reproduce the terms of order, to render the oppressed and marginalized masses available for governing only in a different way than they had been used to. Indeed, political and economic "power," as measured by the extant terms of order, were for King mere "ingredients in the objective that we seek in life." And that ultimate end or objective, King said, was something closer to a "truly brotherly society" or "the creation of the beloved community."[31]

Though he recognized the utilitarian promise of the state, King sought to cure what H. L. T. Quan has referred to as our chronic "state addiction." King fought against the "singular obsession with how we shall be governed." He wanted us to see that "democratic living, as a way of collectivizing, concerns itself not with how we shall be governed, but with how we shall relate to one another."[32] To be sure, King's vision of the beloved community remained anchored in some idea of love as an ordering principle. "A simple working definition," Walter Fluker writes, "is a community ordered by love."[33] But King's notion of the beloved community signaled a profound gesture beyond the ordering logic of the political, beyond the presumption of sovereignty, authority, and hierarchical leadership. It was in many ways an attempt to move beyond state management of governed constituencies. King imagined "a society of friends, a colloquy of equals, a practice of concern, caring, and giving—in which each person had standing, each stone in place, none rejected, in a rising tumult of aspiring mutuality."[34] This was an appeal, if not to a tumultuous disorder akin to what Robinson called the *antipolitical*, at least to a way of collectivizing and relating to one another that would evade the compulsory order of racial capitalist dominion.

Consider how this "rising tumult of aspiring mutuality" applies to the welfarist movements discussed above. The domestic welfare struggles that affected King in the mid-1960s, as well as the later world welfare initiatives that his thinking can be said to have anticipated, were at once political and antipolitical. They were as much an appeal to the state as a governing instrument as they were a challenge to the very presumption of governability. In their political appeal qua claimants, welfare rights activists in the United States sought to render an entire segment of the population essentially unavailable for governing. Their political claim thus reflected what Quan calls a "willful refusal to be governed as confirmation of a democratic sensibility."[35] That is, in this case, a refusal to allow social-reproductive work, indeed a refusal to allow the lives of predominately Black and Latina women, to remain the expropriated dominion of racial and gendered capitalism. On the international stage, world welfare appeals to the United Nations General Assembly, to the redistributive promise of the NIEO, sought to render peoples of the postcolonial Global South essentially unavailable to neocolonial dominion.

King, for his part, stressed how resistance movements from below tend to forge a "new kind of togetherness," as he put it in "Showdown."[36] He was

conscious of this phenomenon during every phase of his struggle and leaned
heavily on its promise in preparation for the Poor People's Campaign, which
was to be much more than a mobilization of claimants making a conventional
"call on the government." The point we are trying to make is that in the process of working within a conventional, state-centric conception of the political, King began to expose the contingency of that very conception. His more
imaginative and creative gestures toward a "new kind of togetherness" worked
to expose the political as the "dominating myth of our consciousness of being
together." This more expansive effort is in its own way antipolitical, as Robinson points out. It serves both to defend against the "destructive objectivation of
the myth," namely, "the apparatuses of repression and control," and "to subvert
that way of realizing" collective life. The key, Robinson says, is to hone the
"ability to hold onto the consciousness that the political is an historical, one
temporarily convenient, illusion."[37] And in King's life and work, this ability to
hold on to such critical consciousness is of course bolstered by his theism, his
Afro-Christian faith in the coming of another world. In grasping for something else, for the transcendent truth and justice of the beloved community,
the illusory, temporal, and thus fleeting nature of the political is thrown into
bolder relief.

Vincent Harding recalls of his comrade that in the last years especially, King
"was slowly turning away from the New Deal–inspired dream that the federal
government (locked as it was into a deadly alliance with an almost autonomous
military and with the U.S.A.-based transnational corporate structures) had any,
or desired any, compassionate solutions—regardless of the color, gender, or political leanings of the president, regardless of which of our major parties was 'in
power.'" Nor was King "inclined to jump to the conclusion that any socialism
that we have seen anywhere offered an alternative model for the 'reconstruction'" of modern society.[38] For King, Harding recalls, "the answers, the models,
the hopes, the new constructions were still in the hearts and minds of all those
men and women who were being drawn away from the old and working their
lives toward a new way" and "*he knew instinctively,* and said it more and more
clearly, that we would be unfaithful to *our own best history of struggle* and to the
hopes of the exploited peoples of the world, if black folk in the U.S.A. were to
settle for what is now called 'a fair share' (and what was known in the sixties
as a 'piece of the pie')—some proportionate cut of the wealth amassed by this
nation's military-industrial empire."[39] To be sure, King "was unclear about how
this would be done." But such was precisely the point. He was "improvising," as
Harding put it, "in the great black tradition."[40]

"A Wholesome, Vibrant Negro Self-Confidence . . ."

Recovery of King's two conceptions of the political puts us in position finally to situate King within the Black radical tradition.[41] The book's broader analytical framework, the theory of racial capitalism, emerged from Robinson's account of this very tradition. Previous chapters have touched on aspects of its ontology and epistemology. But we have not yet trained focus on what Robinson identifies as the tradition's defining nature—namely, its striking, almost incomprehensible aversion to mass violence. Robinson documents how, time and again, in their historical struggles against racial capitalism's dominion, Black people "seldom employed the level of violence that they (the Westerners) understood the situation required."[42] At issue is a philosophy and practice of nonviolent resistance that is to be distinguished from appropriations of European political radicalism, including the violence of "Fanon's extended Freudianism" and the "revolutionary terror" of various Black neo-Marxisms.[43] The resonances with King are profound, both in terms of King's normative philosophy of nonviolence and his descriptive accounts of Black struggle: "the amazing thing," he said in "Showdown," is that "but for a rare exception," Black people "haven't killed any white people, and Negroes could, if they wished, kill by the hundreds."[44] In reconstructing King's two conceptions of the political, in exposing how he worked both within and beyond the governing violence of the state-centered paradigm, we are able to add further perspective to King's own philosophy and practice of nonviolence, which has been otherwise widely studied and remains perhaps the most celebrated dimension of his life and legacy.

First it will be helpful to review the ontological and epistemological claims at the heart of the Black radical tradition. The absence of mass violence in the context of Black liberation struggle—so strange and irrational by Western standards—is a testament to how "a very different and shared order of things" tended to prevail among a "brutally violated people." Robinson traces the vast history of this. Our concern is with the theory that Robinson articulates, and its normative implications. The key ontological claim is that the Black radical tradition demonstrates a "renunciation of actual being for historical being," a denial of extant reality born of a struggle for "the preservation of the ontological" or "integral totality of the people themselves."[45] That is, the Black radical tradition reflects a struggle to retain, or perhaps to retain the possibility of, a form or forms of collective being, of ideas and practices of shared Black life, that are denied or negated by the expectations and requirements of Western modernity—its slavery, its imperialism, its racial capitalism.

In some sense, this would appear to be a backward-facing or conservative orientation: Black liberation as recovery of precapitalist modes of living and being
together. But the argument is much closer to the one that W. E. B. Du Bois
pioneered in "Conservation of Races." Du Bois, whom Robinson identifies as an
exemplary figure in the Black radical tradition, argued for the preservation of a
set of distinctive Black racial "ideals," including a commitment to some notion
of shared living and togetherness, perhaps even a community ordered by love.
This is less about resurrecting a romanticized African past or recovering some
sort of lost communalism than it is about resisting the foreclosure of democratic
and communal possibilities moving forward, in the face of what Du Bois called
"white world" ideals and practices—including abrasive ideologies of competitive
market individualism and the violent partitioning of the racial capitalist order.[46]

What would it mean to "renounce actual being" and thereby "preserve" the
"integral totality" of a people in movement for their liberation? This question
implies a renunciation of the political as a mode of ordering Black lives. We have
spoken about the state as an abstract structure of authority, but Robinson argues
that the political often expresses itself well beyond the purview of the state, in
and through a more pervasive application of a hierarchical leadership ideal in
which the people are essentially called into being and ordered from above. According to this ideal, the led—the masses, the people—are rationalized, comprehended, governed, managed, all at the hands of an exceptional and heroic
individual or body of governing elites. Robinson contrasts this sharply with how
leadership manifested itself in the Black radical tradition, where, he says, it was
more often "an expression of the people focused onto one of their members."[47]
And this, indeed, is where Robinson situates King:

> King's charismatic authority was a tributary of the Afro-Christian tradi-
> tion embedded in the consciousness of the now mostly urban Blacks in
> the South and elsewhere. His leadership was grounded on culturally ce-
> mented legitimacy rather than organizational management skills, on the
> biblical faith tales retold at thousands of places of worship each Sunday, the
> militant millenarianism of Afro-Christian hymns, and the messianism of
> the Gospel. When he spoke, his speech rhythms and language conspired
> with beliefs, concepts, ideas, and icons insinuated into Black Christian
> consciousness for generations. He clarioned a call to action that was heard
> wherever Afro-Christians could be found. . . . In this performance, he was
> less a person than a signature of a social and historical identity. King artic-
> ulated a Salvationist vision of a future but accessible utopia, a golden place

whose every ethical and moral stone was familiar to this widely dispersed congregation. Baker and others, whose genius rested in organization and the analyses of social process, recognized both King's unquestioned authority and his obvious limitations. Baker was appalled by the other SCLC leaders' deference to and dependency on King. But they too were hedged in by the prescripted narrative of Black salvationism. Thus while a Baker or an Abernathy or a Clark might provide organizational integument—that is, practical planning and realistic goals to King's paradigmatic talk—the power of the movement came from the masses, from a century or two of their ancestors, under acute distress, elaborating a vision of the future and how it might be attained. In King they saw their own reflection, not their master, their own ambitions, not his dictates.[48]

The point, we might say, is that King was a man of the people, an expression of its being. Such phrasing has become a grand cliché, of course, and its application in King's case is certainly a vast oversimplification—and a blatant evasion of King's patriarchy.[49] But in King's case there is a real and distinctively Black radical substance to it. King was raised in the Black Church, in the Black working-class milieu that was "Little Africa."[50] As his career moved though formal schooling, through the ministry, ultimately into the role of grand mobilizer of a mass movement, his travel regimen was unrivaled, such that no matter how much his star ascended in the public consciousness, he was still gripped by the plight of urban youth as he moved though Newark and Chicago and Watts, still brought to tears at the sight of starving Black children in rural Mississippi.[51] In the very last year of his life, he was moved by welfare rights activists to "look to them for guidance" and a richer understanding of state violence toward poor Black women.[52] In his final weeks in Memphis, moved by the responsiveness of the Black working class, he spontaneously called for a general strike, what amounts to a movement by a people to forge itself through a grand refusal to be governed.[53] The point is that King was never walled off from the history and present of life-and-death struggles for Black survival. There is something in King—in his leadership, his authority—that is expressive of an African people that had fought for generations to preserve itself as an "integral totality," and not simply as the negation or antithesis of capitalist modernity.

The epistemological claim merits review as well. It has been said that the Black radical tradition denotes "a praxis that can provide an alternative mode of being *and of conducting critical social inquiries*."[54] Robinson describes it as an "accretion, over generations, of *collective intelligence* gathered from struggle."[55]

Part of what it means to "preserve the ontological totality" is to preserve modes of registering, documenting, and disseminating its knowledge. Robinson warns against New World "thefts of consciousness," which he says are equally as tragic as "thefts of labor, life, and material wellbeing."[56] Black scholarship can easily replicate the division between mental and manual labor and become, as Erica Edwards puts it, all too complicit in "the theft of Black being."[57] King's own scholarly training was in many ways conventionally Western, his fondness for the likes of Kant, Hegel, and Marx perhaps complicit in theft. His conventional conception of the political was likewise shaped by exposure to white theologians such as Walter Rauschenbusch and Reinhold Niebuhr, who gave King a "a detailed theological underpinning that supported the need for the state as a principle of order."[58] Gary Dorrien lists an appeal to the state as among the influences that the Black social gospel tradition took from "white social gospel and progressive movements," which "conceived the federal government as an indispensable guarantor of constitutional rights and principles of justice."[59] But Dorrien goes on to add that as King, for his part, became "increasingly radical and angry as a consequence of failing to break white supremacy," he "spurned his access to the establishment in order to stand with the poor and oppressed, struggling against intertwined forms of racial, social, economic, cultural, and imperial oppression."[60] In other words, King did not allow himself to be walled off from the fullness of Black being. His epistemology did not replicate the separation of mental from manual labor that, since Aristotle, has been used by Western elites to legitimize their knowledge claims over slaves and working people.

Consider King's 1968 tribute to Du Bois. "He was in the first place a teacher," King said of Du Bois, who taught that "Black people have been kept in oppression and deprivation by a poisonous fog of lies."[61] For King, Du Bois's most important book, *Black Reconstruction in America*, "demolished the lies about Negroes in their most important and creative period of history," debunked the revisionism of "white historians" to reveal the truth about the "only period in which democracy existed in the South. This stunning fact was the reason the history books had to lie because to tell the truth would have acknowledged the Negroes' capacity to govern and fitness to build a finer nation in a creative relationship with poor whites."[62] Working through the fog of lies and the theft of Black being is what yields "a wholesome, vibrant Negro self-confidence"—not only in the sense of recovering the dignity of self that had been beaten down by slavery and Jim Crow, both old and new, but also in the sense of promoting the self-confidence of the Black world: the ideas, values, principles, and defining natures that the ontological totality stands for.

To be sure, it can be tempting to read the epistemological dimension of the Black radical tradition as something of a flight into idealism. Robinson himself acknowledges this when he says that "its epistemology granted supremacy to metaphysics not the material," and that Black radical alternatives to the political were often "translated and transformed into ethical theory, theology, and philosophy, that is into forms of idealism."[63] There is more than a grain of this in King's notion of the beloved community, which owes much to the mysticism of Howard Thurman and Afro-Christian spirituality.[64] But the Black radical tradition complicates any binary distinction between ideal and real. In the struggle for survival, the limitations and perversions of the white world become intelligible, as do both real and speculative gestures toward alternative possibilities of being and living together. Despite all the dehumanization, despite all the reason to despair, writes George Lipsitz, Black people "somehow managed to extend recognition and respect to each other while in bondage, and to maintain a commitment to the linked fate of all humans, [and they] countered vicious dehumanization with determined and successful re-humanization. Insisting on their own humanity and the humanity of all people, even that of their oppressors, they have been at the forefront of what Dr. King called 'the bitter but beautiful struggle' for a more just and better world."[65]

Our focus on King's two concepts of the political helps both to situate King within the Black radical tradition and to cast new light on his theory and practice of nonviolence. Again, it is the relative absence of mass violence that Robinson identifies as the defining nature of the tradition. King's commitment to nonviolence is part of an effort to vivify—or, as he would say in "Showdown" and elsewhere, "dramatize"—the violence of racial capitalism and the statist paradigm. This is perhaps his grand contribution to Black study, a testament to his refusal to produce or reproduce knowledge that is complicit in the theft of Black being. But his commitment to nonviolence can also be read to reconcile the layered nature of his political theory, or to bridge his movement through the two concepts of the political.

The key is that nonviolence augurs a democratic praxis, both as means and as end. Within the conventional paradigm of the statist order, as exploited and expropriated communities struggle to win state recognition of their formal and informal labors, nonviolence is the most effective means of pressuring the state from below. King knew that Black communities would never win gun battles with the U.S. government. And he feared white backlash to demonstrations of violent resistance and insurrection, what he said in "Showdown for Nonviolence" could quickly descend into a "right-wing takeover" and "Fascist development" that would foreclose democratic possibility.[66] If "legitimacy" in the era of state-managed capitalism depends upon some working consensus of popular support, then nonviolence is necessary (a) to expand popular concern about a legitimacy crisis—that is, concern about the extent to which Black and poor people continue to be exploited, expropriated, and disposed of, despite the historically expanded societal capacity to overcome this—and (b) to draw on that heightened concern to forge a multiracial consensus that could realistically pressure the state to overcome and deliver on its expanded capacity.[67] In this way, as Karuna Mantena has argued, King gave us a "theory and a practice of nonviolence that were conceptually realist and intensely pragmatic, and that aimed at making visible the moral stakes of undoing racial domination."[68] Racial progress for King "depended on finding a way to get every American to see themselves personally implicated in racial domination," and "nonviolence was the best means to *persuade* a reluctant populace to actively engage in acts of moral reevaluation."[69] Mantena refers specifically to the American context, but inference suggests that King intended this logic to apply beyond national borders.

The transnational context allows for an even more vivid rendering of how King regarded nonviolence as much more than simply an effective means of working within the statist paradigm. To be sure, King kept one foot planted in the model of "national salvation," wedded as he was to the notion that the representative nation-state was the established institutional arrangement that could potentially facilitate some measure of democratic responsiveness, where other existing modes of coordination, most principally the market economy, could not. But the ultimate end or objective, as we have seen, was the human togetherness that is forged in the struggle, the building of community, the real democratic substance of it all. King would not pursue violent resistance, he would not pursue strategies or ends of racial separatism in the United States, in part because he knew that racialized groups would have to continue to engage one another in the wake of any bloodletting. He wanted racialized groups to continue to engage one another, albeit in radically transformed ways—that is, peacefully, productively, sustainably.[70] Beyond the borders of the United States, in the context of postwar anti-colonial struggle, the "national salvation" model may have lent itself more easily to ideas about violent resistance and insurrection, if only because it was both possible and necessary to push out the colonizer, to restore land and control to native peoples, rather than to *persuade* settlers and natives to engage in shared governance within the borders of the postcolony. But here, too, King knew that postcolonial regimes would have to continue to engage external peoples and states in the broader global arena. And if there was ever going to be any hope of moving beyond an international politics mired in national interest and transactional exchange relationships between territorial states, if there was to be any hope of moving beyond the reproduction of North-South asymmetries and relationships of domination and dependency, then some sort of global democratic togetherness would need to take shape. It was and remains something of an otherworldly—Robinson might say "outlandish"—proposition.[71] But King was not willing to foreclose the possibility.

"To Meet the Future with a Clear Conscience . . ."

King lived through an era of state-managed capitalism. The contradictions of that era have since given way to the neoliberal present, a moment in which global capital (particularly finance capital) and the transnational private sector have in many ways captured the governing capacity of territorial states. Where King saw promise in a more democratically accountable state apparatus that could rein in capital, at least to some degree, and forestall its tendency to decimate labor, exacerbate inequalities, and essentially cannibalize itself, the very successes of that model prompted a tremendous backlash on the part of the ownership class, such that in the fifty years since King's death, we find ourselves forced to reimagine the relationship between polity and economy that the social welfare contract presupposes. We argue that King's liminal standing between two conceptions of the political—again, the conventional, state-centric model on one flank, and a more Black radical democratic praxis on the other—suggests a way of reckoning with the neoliberal condition.

On one flank is the imperative to recover popular political control over the economy and to restore a commitment to the welfare and developmental state. Welfare reform efforts in the United States in the 1960s were imperfect and limited in their capacity to transform basic structural features of the economy. So, too, were the world welfare initiatives at the global level. But as Reverend William J. Barber's renewed Poor People's Campaign attests, it still makes desperate sense to, as King put it, "plague Congress," to "plague the government, until they will do something," until "the nation will not be able to overlook the poor."[72] Such an approach may be more limited today, given the relative incapacity of the U.S. government or any other territorial state to reverse the direction of capture, to restore some degree of management of the sheer force of global capital.[73] Nancy Fraser has argued that in working in this vein today, it is useful to shift categories of analysis and prescription. Instead of attempting to negotiate a relation between polity and economy, instead of focusing on the state management of capital, it may be more appropriate and generative to think in terms of a re-empowerment of the public vis-à-vis the private power of capital.[74] The real imperative, after all, is not to empower the *state*, but to protect and enable the *publics* that states have the capacity to serve. We spoke in chapter two about how King's legacy jells with Michael Dawson's call to dismantle neoliberalism though a rebuilding of the "Black counterpublic."[75] That aspect of King's legacy is reaffirmed here as an expression of a conventionally political prescription, albeit one that decenters and destabilizes the political itself.

It does so in part by shifting focus toward racial capitalism's backstory. The rise of the Black radical counterpublic necessarily challenges the ways in which the state confers and manages racial subjections, which have been and remain central to the reproduction and legitimation of the inequalities that capital accumulation requires. To compel the state to recognize and compensate expropriated Black labor, for example, including the social-reproductive work of Black women, or to compel the state to confront its ongoing enforcement of racial partition through residential segregation, is to move toward a restructuring of the very society that gave rise to the political. Remember, "the political came to fruition," Robinson said, "with the theory of the State as the primary vehicle for the organization and ordering of the mass society produced by capitalism." If there is mass resistance among those who are meant to be ordered, among those whom capitalism exploits and expropriates and divides and conquers, then the political is necessarily destabilized. In this regard, King's work with the original Poor People's Campaign, and what that could have become, is exemplary. It has been said of his last campaign that "King knew what he needed to do and with whom he needed to be," and that "he only did not know where this was heading politically."[76]

Robinson might have said that King was heading away from the political, that social movements of this sort are in their own way *antipolitical*. They have the effect of exposing the "mythical" nature of the political and its terms of order. In a neoliberal moment, the *antipolitical* exposure of myth requires, perhaps most significantly, a reckoning with market fundamentalism. Capitalism's neoliberal phase has amplified the tendency of all capitalist societies to defer to "market forces" collective decisions about how to invest society's "surplus"—what Fraser, following Marx, calls the "collective fund of social energies exceeding those required to reproduce a given form of life and to replenish what is used up in the course of living it." Fraser adds that "how a society uses its surplus capacities is absolutely central, raising fundamental questions about how people want to live—where they choose to invest their collective energies, how they propose to balance 'productive work' vis-à-vis family life, leisure and other activities—as well as how they aspire to relate to non-human nature and what they aim to leave to future generations."[77] These are not questions about how we want to be governed. They are not conventionally *political* questions. They are, rather, questions about how we want to live, how we want to be together in the world. And these questions are not restricted to the context of what we might think of as local or domestic societies; the manner in which racial capitalism today compels the absorption of surplus—as a movement away from reinvestment in productive output and toward predatory and extractive financialization—is necessarily a global phenomenon. At a time when the private power of capital has captured territorial states worldwide, rolled back the welfare state contract in the rich countries and the developmental state model at the periphery, compelled state actors everywhere to consider and pursue only "market solutions," we point to King's democratic praxis, the *antipolitical* flank of his political theoretical imaginary, as a refusal to be governed.

CHAPTER FIVE

"Liberated Grounds on Which to Gather"

On Black Study and the Afterlives of King's Critique

Physically and ideologically, and for rather unique historical reasons, African peoples bridge the decline of one world order and the eruption (we may surmise) of another. It is a frightful and uncertain space of being. If we are to survive, we must take nothing that is dead and choose wisely from among the dying.

—Cedric J. Robinson,
Black Marxism: The Making of the Black Radical Tradition

An embattled, colonized people need liberated grounds on which to gather, to reflect, to teach, to learn, to publish, to move towards self-definition and self-determination. Some of these grounds may be in the heart of contemporary white-controlled institutions, but the experiences of the past few years indicate that there are far fewer grounds in such places than we would like to believe. . . . The vast majority of the black institutions we need are yet to be born. To live the truth is to join in the process of that birth, of that building.

—Vincent Harding, "The Vocation of the Black Scholar
and the Struggles of the Black Community"

K ING'S ASSASSINATION IS FREQUENTLY TAKEN to mark the end of a nonviolent, reformist-oriented movement and the beginning of the more militant Black Power era. As Brandon Terry has shown, this framing oversimplifies the intensely complicated "problem-space" of the late 1960s and overdetermines the relationship between the radical dimensions of King's life and work and the direction of Black politics in subsequent decades.[1]

This framing also obscures the historical struggle over King's legacy. At issue are important questions not only about how we remember one of the most noted personalities in modern history, but also about how, faced with the persistence of Black suffering more than a half century on, we might revisit the missed opportunities that King's legacy represents.

In this chapter we consider a lesser-known claim on King's legacy, that of Vincent Harding and the Institute of the Black World (IBW), in an effort to reflect on the institutional spaces that nurture the critique of racial capitalism. King was a student of the Black world. And part of what it means to carry forth his legacy is to pick up on lines of inquiry, to wrestle with his thinking about the prospects and pitfalls of the Black freedom struggle, to reconstruct the critical theories that undergirded his vision and assess their explanatory power, and to part with and move beyond King where necessary. Harding, who had been a professor of history at Spelman College since 1965 and helped to author King's famous 1967 antiwar speech, sought to facilitate this aspect of the King legacy, in part, by working with a group of Black academics to establish the IBW in Atlanta shortly after King's death. Rooted in an avowed commitment to "the colonized situation of the masses of the black community," the IBW was to be a center of Black studies, ecumenical in orientation and focused, as King was, on working out higher syntheses of diverse ideological perspectives.[2] Initially affiliated with the Martin Luther King Memorial Center, the IBW unsettled the Center's philanthropic backing and quickly wore out that partnership. Mindful of the pitfalls of the liberal democratic establishment, Harding and his comrades sought to cultivate the Black radical counterpublic. Part of this entailed, as he put it in 1974, a principled commitment to the "vocation of the black scholar" and an unflinching courage to identify and speak truth to the enemy. "Nothing that is black and whole and alive in America can be fully comprehended apart from the endless white thrusts towards our exploitation, deracination, death, and dismemberment," Harding said. "No discussion of schools or banks, of black mayors or black production workers, of black music or black literature, of black politics or black religion in America can make sense to the people unless we identify the enemy."[3] For Harding, that meant identifying systems of oppression, the complex and often secretive ways in which racial capitalism spreads its tentacles everywhere, including into the institutional spaces that are intended to nurture its critique.

The IBW, established very deliberately to carry forth a mode of Black scholarship in the spirit of King's later work, presents a case study in the challenges, both epistemic and material, of planning and building the beloved community from within the confines of the racial capitalist world order. The IBW's roster included the likes of Stephen Henderson, William Strickland, Lerone Bennett, Howard Dodson, Walter Rodney, Sylvia Wynter, C. L. R. James, Ella Baker, James and Grace Lee Boggs, Katherine Dunham, George Beckford, St. Clair Drake, and Ossie Davis, among others. "The depth and variety of scholar-activists at the IBW made it the greatest collection of black intellectual talent in post–World War II America," writes the historian Derrick White.[4] But—or perhaps precisely because of this—the Institute was chronically underfunded, infiltrated by both the FBI and local police, and held at a distance by the leadership of the Black colleges and universities with which it was marginally affiliated. It was a short-lived experiment, forced into closure by the early 1980s. In what follows, drawing on Harding's "The Vocation of the Black Scholar and the Struggles of the Black Community" as our anchor, we explore how the trappings of the post–civil rights milieu shaped efforts to carve out institutional space for critical Black research and scholarship. We consider how the demands of professionalization, managerialism, policy prescription, and philanthropic funding undermine the work.

These considerations invite comparison with contemporary debates about institutional support for Black studies. At a time when teaching, learning, and scholar-activism have become almost entirely circumscribed by neoliberal rationality and a structural dependency on both the state and private capital, some have sought to theorize a mode of Black study that is "in but not of" formally established institutions—most notably the predominately white university.[5] The idea is not to try to build independent Black institutions, nor to press for more governing control over predominately white spaces, perhaps owing to a certain pessimism about the viability or prospects of such efforts. Instead, transgressive Black study is seen as a mode of flight into what Stefano Harney and Fred Moten refer to as the university's "undercommons." This is a necessarily fugitive act of "[sneaking] into the university" to "steal what one can."[6] Perhaps the closure of the IBW was a historical inevitability, a testament to the suffocating grip of racial capitalist dominion. But as we think about transformative Black study as a mode of flight in the twenty-first century, perhaps the time has come again to look beyond familiar and established institutions, to reimagine the IBW as a missed opportunity, and to recommit to the work of building.

"Indissoluble Bonds to the Heaving Life of the Black Masses . . ."

Harding and the IBW began from the presumption of an "embattled, colonized people." The internal colonialism thesis, which King himself subscribed to in his last years, vivifies both the complexity of racial-capitalist domination and concerns about replicating its formations in and through critique and political practice. Any mode of Black study that could hope to "avoid the realities of white racist-capitalist exploitation of the black community" would need to guard against absorption into neocolonial management schemes, including the emergent custodial politics of the post–civil rights era.[7] This necessarily involves, as IBW affiliate Walter Rodney put it in 1969, a mode of scholar-activism that "attaches [itself] to the activity of the black masses" or that reflects, in Harding's words, "indissoluble bonds to the heaving life of the black masses."[8] Harding and his IBW associates were concerned about how the temptations of the post–civil rights era—the allure of individualized access, "talk of 'making it' in the system"—were being made to crowd out critical scholarship and sustained "movement against the white mainstream." But such "surface manifestations," Harding said, "are never the best indication of the movement of the black community," where "critical repositioning" is always already underway.[9] The vocation of the Black scholar, the meaning and purpose of Black study, is to remain grounded in this movement from below. None of this was new or innovative. The IBW's vision for a critique evoked from the "searing life" of the frontline bearers of racial capitalism had long been central to the Black radical tradition.[10]

Throughout the twentieth century, it had been the relatively marginalized pedagogical work of Black working people—many of them Black women—who pushed for a "group-centered" cultivation of ideas. Here it is worth highlighting the work of Ella Baker, the Student Nonviolent Coordinating Committee (and onetime SCLC) organizer who famously tied grassroots education to a de-hierarchical model of movement leadership. Disaffected by the "hero-worship" that trailed King throughout at least his first phase, Baker stressed that any social movement that belittled, wittingly or not, the desires and wishes of ordinary people risked undercutting the epistemic and material power of democratic struggle. We have seen how King can be read to align with and reflect a kind of deference to the Black masses, but it is Baker, much more than King, who really vivifies a faith in the people's capacity to study and to educate collective movement by virtue of their ability to judge critically the situations in which they find themselves.[11]

Baker was especially well positioned to expose the pitfalls of structured hierarchies in the context of grassroots education and inquiry. Her activist career had long been oriented to cooperative politics. She spent the early part of the 1930s organizing with the Young Negroes' Cooperative League (YNCL), an organization that aspired to build Black economic power through collective planning. Central to that work, as Barbara Ransby has shown, was a practice of training understood as the fortifying of intellectual tools that could flow into, as Baker put it, "self-directed action" against capitalism. Of course Baker was ever mindful of the ways in which white supremacism had been integrally tied to the capitalist mode of production. As Ransby puts it, she "recognized the historical significance of racism as the cornerstone of an unjust social and economic order in the United States extending back to slavery." A "movement for black freedom, defined broadly, she thought, would inevitably be a movement against economic exploitation and the oppressive conditions faced by other groups within American society as well."[12]

In 1936, Baker went to work for the Works Progress Administration's Worker Education Project, focusing her efforts on labor education and encouraging Black workers to "not be satisfied with things as they are" and instead "see the world as theirs and from which they have a right to take what rightfully belongs to them." For Baker, it was necessary to organize not only at the points of production and distribution, but also at the point of consumption. As she put it in a syllabus on consumer education disseminated for the Project, "The wage-earner's well-being is determined as much at the points of distribution and consumption as at the point of production." And because "recurrent 'business slumps' and the increased mechanization of industry tend to decrease the primal importance of the worker as producer," working people "must be oriented to the increasingly more important role of consumer."[13] This falls in line with a broadly left vision, one plainly shared by King, of an economy driven not by profit and private ownership, but rather by an attentiveness to human needs. But more to our point, for Baker—as for King, Harding, and others of the Black radical tradition—the full breadth of the epistemic critique is shaped by the lived realities of the Black masses, wherever and however they may live, work, and consume.

Emergent here is a powerful retort to the generalized distrust of the Black poor and working class, which is so pronounced in managerial configurations of Black politics. Robert Gooding-Williams has shown that one attempt to avoid replicating a ruler-centered politics, which in this case is premised on the assumption of a need to reform or modernize "culturally backward" Black masses, is to declare a kind of independence, and thereby position oneself to imagine the possibility of its abolition.[14] We might say that Baker and a whole cast of intellectuals and activists concerned with grassroots education sought to declare independence from racial capitalism's terms of order, from its hierarchies, from the presumption of governability. Baker would insist in 1964, the year that she and other SNCC organizers helped to establish over fifty Freedom Schools in Mississippi, that "we want to bring the student to a point where he questions everything he reads or is taught—the printed word, movies, the 'power structure'—everything."[15]

This orientation was the heart and soul of many efforts to institutionalize grassroots education, including those undertaken at the Highlander Folk School in Tennessee. Myles Horton, the legendary labor organizer who founded the school in the 1930s, stressed the need for a radical break with the terms of order. "Most people don't allow themselves to experiment with ideas, because they assume that they have to fit into the system," he said in a dialogue with the radical educator and philosopher Paolo Freire just before his death. "They say how can I live out these things I believe in within the capitalist system, within the subsystem of capitalism, the microcosm of capitalism, the school system and within the confines of respectability, acceptance. Consequently, they don't allow themselves to think of any other way of doing things."[16] To be sure, at its core Highlander was, according to historian David Levine, "unabashedly convinced that 'ordinary people' possess the power to transform themselves as they work to transform the society in which they live."[17] Highlander educator and "Mother of the Movement" Septima Clark stressed that the mission was to "see people as they see themselves and to help generate within them the desires and determination to improve their conditions."[18] But for our purposes, the point is that all of this requires a push for autonomy, independence, separation, flight from the structures and strictures of extant thought and experience. And this push for what Harding would call "liberated grounds on which to gather" is profoundly complicated by the historical embeddedness of formally institutionalized spaces for grassroots teaching, learning, and scholarship.

King's involvement with Highlander is a case in point. He traveled to Tennessee in 1957 to give the closing address at Highlander's twenty-fifth anniversary seminar. There he praised Highlander for its "dauntless courage and fearless determination," drew out connections between the civil rights and labor movements, and closed with his signature call for "maladjustment"—essentially a mode of flight from the world as we have come to know and experience it.[19] The session was infiltrated by the FBI. King was labeled a heretic and a communist. For years the right wing had sought to brand Highlander a "communist training school."[20] Tennessee state officials revoked Highlander's charter in 1961 and forced the operation to flee to the mountains. Its work lived on. As the Poor People's Campaign moved ahead following King's death, for example, Highlander was right there on the front lines, holding workshops with the people, training foot soldiers in the fight against poverty and dispossession. But for Harding and those intent on carrying on this dimension of King's legacy, the call for institutional autonomy had reached a crescendo.

"Possession by the Truth ..."

The IBW was conceived as an "experiment in black responsibility for that intellectual work which defines and directs the black community." Its "Statement of Purpose" fashioned a call to action in reference to King's stirring tribute to another Black scholar-activist who had been branded a heretic and a communist, and who ultimately had been compelled to flee the country in an effort to gain some much-needed distance. "We dare to experiment," the IBW statement read, "partly because we remember the words spoken by Martin Luther King, Jr., one year before his assassination, as he memorialized W. E. B. Du Bois. Dr. King said then: 'It was never possible to know where the scholar Du Bois ended and the organizer Du Bois began. The two qualities in him were a single unified force.'"[21] Also noted in King's tribute was another driving theme of the IBW's purpose, namely, the pursuit of truth, a commitment to the principle that what it means to give oneself over to Black study is to break through a "poisonous fog of lies."[22]

In "Vocation," Harding said that "there are few better summaries of our calling: to speak truth to our people, to speak truth about our people, to speak truth about our enemy—all in order to free the mind, so that black men, women, and children may build beyond the banal, dangerous chaos of the American spirit, towards a new time."[23] He also stressed, in what we now might recognize as a classic formulation in the Black radical tradition, that this requires a fundamental reworking of how we understand possession and property, indeed how we understand our embeddedness within racial capitalist society. "We are finally driven to remember our selves, to recollect our beings, to know that our deepest origins have little to do with American style, but are to be found in a series of cultures in which much emphasis is often placed on the living, acting, dancing, *performing* of the truth. Indeed, we come from great bodies of men and women who have for many centuries experienced what is fittingly known as possession by the truth. . . . Everyone who has ever observed or experienced possession in African peoples knows that it is not in any way respectable by American standards."[24] Drawing on ancestral memory in renouncing "actual being for historical being," forging a "revolutionary consciousness . . . from the whole historical experience of Black people and not merely from the social formations of capitalist slavery or the relations of production of colonialism," anticipating a mode of Black study that is "in but not of," Harding envisioned a Black institution that flatly rejects possession as property by racial capital and the neocolonial state, an institution that refuses to be owned and controlled. What he had in mind, rather, was an institution that is possessed by the truth, a Black institution that is, as Fanon put it in his final days, "slave to a cause."[25]

Robinson, for his part, characterized it as "a frightful and uncertain space of being," this liminal mode of passage "bridg[ing] the decline of one world order and the eruption (we may surmise) of another."[26] Harding said that it takes tremendous courage to enter this space and a willingness to disavow any notion of respectability. "Becoming personally involved in the concrete, active struggle for liberation, entering deeply into its life, and opening our own lives to its risks, is, of course, the most unrespectable aspect of the vocation."[27] One way to approach consideration of the material challenges involved in building an institution such as the IBW is to focus on the battle over the "respectability" of King's legacy and its public-and private-sector financial sponsors. The post–civil rights electoral class and white liberal philanthropy fought very hard to fashion King as a paragon of liberal respectability. They provided at least some semblance of material support for institutions that would carry on the narrowest claims of King's first-phase civil rights liberalism and carefully shut out those, such as the IBW, that saw a deeper truth in King's struggle to expose the unrespectable underbelly of racial capitalism.[28]

In his 1969 book, *Black Awakening in Capitalist America*, Robert Allen raised alarm over white philanthropic interests that sought to invest in a range of Black-led organizations with the intent of filtering acceptable political ideology. As organizations such as the Ford Foundation moved to shape social policy, they became increasingly invested in managing dissent. Under the banner of "public affairs," they prioritized reform over radicalism and sought to stabilize the political and economic order by encouraging the civil society organizations they supported to pursue "peaceful and constructive" solutions to urban unrest and rebellion. Emerging think tanks such as the Metropolitan Applied Research Center (MARC) and the Joint Center for Political Studies (JCSP) began their ascent in the world of shaping Black public opinion just as Ford and other sponsors began shifting their funding priorities to "serve the public need" through such mechanisms as public-private partnerships.[29]

The connections between the stifling of dissent so characteristic of Cold War liberalism and more concealed forms of philanthropic social manipulation were startlingly close. Ford's president from 1966 through the mid-1970s, McGeorge

Bundy, for example, had been a National Security Advisor during the Kennedy Administration and was a chief architect of the U.S. strategy in Vietnam. He believed that the expansion of Ford's social mission was tied to the U.S. imperative to develop and stabilize markets at home and abroad. As Allen noted, "stability and capitalist development are essential to the tranquil internal growth and external expansion of the American empire. Instability and underdevelopment, whether at home or abroad, breed violence and revolution. It is for this reason that by the end of 1966 the Foundation had committed seventy-two million dollars to research in population control in the United States, Britain, Europe, Israel, Australia, Asia, and Latin America. It is for this reason that it devotes approximately one-fifth of its annual budget to training personnel and building economic institutions in underdeveloped countries . . . and it is for this reason that in September 1968, it announced plans to invest an initial ten million dollars in the building of black capitalism."[30] It would appear that the point of philanthropic investment in Black movements was to muddy the waters of Black dissent by rendering unimaginable the idea that the substantive shape of those very movements could operate outside the terms of the liberal consensus. The point, clearly, was to manage the Black masses.

If philanthropic organizations had embarked on a massive campaign to diversify their capital investments and curtail Black freedom dreams, many Black middle-class elites were willing to oblige. The King Center, of course, split with the IBW less than a year after its founding in 1970, largely over concerns about potential damage to its reputation and ability to attract and retain funding. But the split also highlighted an ideological battle over what political or public-sector support for Black freedom dreams would entail. The King Center's view was informed by a remarkably constrained reading of King's perspective on the conditions of poor and working-class Black people. In place of King's own conclusions that racial partition, disinvestment, and uneven development were structural constraints on Black freedom, the King Center stressed the promise of equal opportunity and the crowning achievements of civil rights–era legislation.[31] But "the broad mass of the black community was no less an internal colony now than in 1965," Harding said a decade later, and the fact that "certain heirs of Martin King" had come to "support of the myth of Black Capitalism as a means to 'Save Humanity'" was nothing short of obscene.[32] The idea that persistent inequalities were simply a kink in an otherwise perfectible system poorly misjudged the depth of the problem and the urgent necessity of more expansive critique. As Harding put it, "the legal and penal system . . . the economic system . . . the healthcare system . . . the energy conservation system . . .

the military . . . and culture" were all trained on the domination of Black and poor people, subjecting them, in one way or another, to vulnerability, suffering, and premature death.[33]

The funding constraints of the liberal consensus and the ownership claims over sponsored research initiatives had a profound impact on the shaping of the political imagination. Consider the case of the Joint Center for Political Studies. JCPS was cofounded in 1970 by the noted Black sociologist Kenneth B. Clark, who in 1965 helped to pioneer the "internal colonialism" thesis. America's "dark ghettoes," he wrote, were "social, political, educational, and—above all—economic colonies," and their inhabitants "subject peoples, victims of the greed, cruelty, insensitivity, guilt, and fear of their masters."[34] Yet the think tank that Clark later founded proffered a program of political managerialism and technocratic policy prescription that remained firmly anchored in the paradigm of the political and its presumptions of hierarchy, order, and governability. Having secured a two-year grant from the Ford Foundation in 1970, JCPS made its commitments clear: "attract increased support from officials, business leaders, foundations, corporations and the general public."[35] *Black Enterprise* noted in a 1978 article on JCPS that Clark's later work leading a New York–based management consulting firm positioned him well as a mediating voice between the governing elite and Black public opinion.[36] It is difficult to imagine how the outcomes of such an approach could be anything other than replication of the very structural relationships that feed the circuits of racial capitalist accumulation.

To be sure, following its initial work on Black studies in 1970-71, the IBW committed to its status as an activist think tank and sought to shape a Black political agenda. But this was never conceived as an exercise in technocratic governance. As Vincent Harding and William Strickland wrote of their "Black political agenda" in *The New York Times* in 1972, "blacks must resist the temptation to trust in [the political] system to bring forth a humane society . . . blacks must move to a politics of profound 'black reconstruction.' . . . Blacks must not only set the agenda, but organize and struggle to achieve it."[37] The IBW's foray into electoral politics—its involvement in the 1972 National Black Political Convention in Gary, Indiana, as well as its support of the first mayoral campaign of Maynard Jackson in Atlanta—led rather quickly to a sense of disillusionment. Shunning what Harding called "politics as usual," stressing what sounded a lot like King's warnings about the pitfalls of political power conceived as an end in itself, Harding stressed that "electoral politics can be a viable *tactic* for liberation," but only "if it is converted from transient political *campaigns* into a *permanent political movement*."[38] In other words, the IBW's Black political agenda remained firmly grounded in the "heaving life of the Black masses." Electoral politics can be useful, but only as an expression of a vibrant, worldmaking movement.

Ultimately the King Center found support for a narrow reading of King, while organizations such as MARC and JCPS developed political agendas in the service of custodial management. In doing so, they set the stage for appropriations of King's vision and for projections of the Black freedom struggle that would become commonplace among white liberals and conservatives, corporate boards, philanthropic organizations, and indeed, the emerging Black political class. As Dylan Rodriguez has argued, the relationship between financial sponsorship and the controlling of political ideology is part and parcel of philanthropic hegemony in which "a set of symbiotic relationships . . . link political and financial technologies of state and owning class control with surveillance over public political ideology, including and especially emergent progressive and leftist social movements."[39] The consequences are profound. The "non-profit industrial complex," Rodriguez has shown, directs social energy into the reproduction of civil society with the expressed purpose of managing social relations and preserving a form of political rule. "The Left's investment in the essential political logic of civil society—specifically, the inherent legitimacy of racist state violence in upholding a white freedom, social 'peace,' and 'law and order' that is fundamentally designed to maintain brutal inequalities in the putative free world—is symbiotic with (and not oppositional to) the policing and incarceration of marginalized, racially pathologized communities, as well as the state's ongoing absorption of organized dissent through the non-profit structure."[40]

The IBW, for its part, was in a tough spot. Senior associate and *Ebony* editor Lerone Bennett argued that while "there is no such thing as pure autonomy or pure black money," the organization could still seek out some form of "relative autonomy."[41] He sought to reinterpret the acceptance of blood money not as indicative of dependency on white philanthropy, but rather as a form of reparative justice paid out by historically dispossessive perpetrators. Still, such philosophical justifications could not liberate the Institute from the discursive song and dance that fundraising required. Following the split with the King Center, staff members were forced to offset declining revenue by taking on additional jobs: paid speaking engagements, freelance work, and in some cases formal teaching appointments at established universities. A direct mailing campaign showed signs of promise, but the returns were always meager. The IBW tried to sell bigger donors on ideological plurality and a "synthesis of leading ideas and ideologies," even as it was clear that their on-the-ground programming involved a less agnostic account of the organization's aspirations. By 1972, the IBW was working in solidarity with prison uprisings and global working-class movements. Associates were hosting grassroots education workshops and directed readings of Amílcar Cabral's *Revolution in Guinea,* Mary Frances Berry's *Black Resistance/White Law,* Allen's *Black Awakening in Capitalist America,* Walter Rodney's *The Groundings with My Brothers,* and Gary Nash's *Red, White, and Black.*[42] Even if the IBW pronounced its "relative autonomy" to engage in unrespectable work, even if the Institute diversified its revenue streams, even if it was not *of* the colonial apparatus and the racial capitalist order, it most certainly operated *in* it. The endowment returns of its charitable sponsors continued to flow through accumulative circuits of dispossession and uneven development. The disciplinary gaze of dependency was constantly reinforced by the possibility that private donors could pull out at any time, for any reason. The legal apparatus of the capitalist state continued to provide protection and enforcement of the accumulative interests of the ownership class. And any white Northern universities that contracted with the IBW to advise and evaluate emerging Black studies programs had certainly gotten rich through the underdevelopment of the Black world. Despite any marginal Black studies initiatives, such schools were set up to continue greasing the gears of racial capitalist inequality.

"The Questionable Freedom and Relative Affluence of the American University . . ."

There was initially some confusion over whether or not the IBW was a school, an aspiring "Black university" of the sort that Harding had theorized in tandem with his efforts to launch the IBW. Harding was a professor of history at Spelman when he—along with Gerald McWorter (later Abdul Alkalimat), a professor of sociology at Spelman, and Stephen Henderson, a professor of Black literature at Morehouse—laid the groundwork for an Institute for Advanced Afro-American Studies at the Atlanta University Center (AUC). This was the precursor to the IBW. As Derrick White has carefully documented, the IBW grew out of the Black studies movement that had roiled college and university campuses nationwide during the late 1960s.[43] Established schools, including the Black colleges in Atlanta, proved to be deeply sedimented and inhospitable to Black studies. This led Harding and his comrades to pursue "relative autonomy" through institutional separation from the university.

To be sure, Harding did see promise in a radical renewal of Black higher education. Harding, McWorter, and others sketched out the concept of the "Black university." In the pages of *Ebony* in 1970, Harding imagined this as "a new place or a renewed institution or a complex of institutions" driven by "an attempt to break with the long-established familiar patterns of white domination and control over black higher education." He imagined a university that would "enter that stream of global anti-colonialism which refuses to educate young people primarily for the service of the colonizers."[44] The Black university had to disavow white American common sense about what colleges and universities are supposed to be. "Dark copies of dying whiteness are no longer needed," he said. It was time for the Black university to break with a dying civilization, to get on the right side of history and demonstrate a "total commitment to the life" of the Black community and world.[45] And he was clear that this was to be something distinct from the IBW, but an initiative that could be supported by it. "While those of us at the Institute of the Black World do not consider ourselves a Black University, we are building a research center which will perhaps help to create the content, direction and materials for those new or re-ordered institutions which have committed themselves in such black directions."[46]

Harding was convinced that experiments at the time, such as the Malcolm X Liberation University in North Carolina, reflected a strong desire for a radically new kind of university.[47] But he was clear that no established Black college or university in 1970 fit the mold. And the battles with administrators over Black studies programs at Morehouse and Spelman led Harding to think, at least initially, that King Center sponsorship would enable a greater degree of institutional autonomy. By the late 1960s, well into the daylight of the Black Power era, AUC administrators, like those at predominately white schools nationwide, were deeply concerned about burgeoning student radicalism and the institutionalization of Black studies on their campuses.[48] A key flashpoint was the 1969 dismissal of Morehouse professor A. B. Spellman, who had been involved in a failed attempt with students to push for a Black-centered curriculum. The student-led *Atlanta University Black Paper* remarked on the episode, calling out the administration's "authoritative, sophisticated force to squelch the thrust of the educational revolution," what the students regarded as little more than an attempt to kowtow "to the interests of the Rockefellers, Fords, DuPonts and Harrimans."[49] For private institutions such as Morehouse and Spelman, structural dependency on white philanthropy made the prospects of radical renewal of the sort that Harding had in mind all but a nonstarter. He suggested that material support for the Black university concept would require claims on the public coffers and a "constant experimentation" with the "still untapped sources of funding within the black community."[50]

When Harding and Henderson officially launched the IBW in January 1970, the organization had no formal affiliation with any college or university. Harding claimed that "for the life and work of the black scholar in search of vocation, the primary context is not to be found in the questionable freedom and relative affluence of the American university, nor in the ponderous uncertainties of 'the scholarly community.'"[51] That relative affluence, as Craig Steven Wilder has shown, was quite literally built on the back of African slave labor.[52] As Abigail Boggs and Nick Mitchell put it, "there is no history of the university that is not also a history of capital accumulation and capital expropriation."[53] Whether we are referring to predominately white or historically Black schools, the American university's mode of sustaining itself "was derived from and inventive of practices and structures of violence and captivity indissociable from the fact of their genesis as slaveholding settler institutions." Though we tend to imagine that education is reducible to instruction, to a nurturing relation between students and teachers, its institutional reality is a "context constituted as much by students and instructors as it is by those who cleared furnace ashes and emptied chamber pots, by those whose communities were removed for campuses to take root, and by those whose bodies were used as the raw materials for scientific experimentation and discursive elaboration alike." On and around today's campuses, and across the global supply chains that serve them, living labor continues to serve dead labor as a means of "accumulation-by-education."[54] An ugly past gives way to a present university that continues these constitutive processes and refines their technologies. Universities remain settler colonial institutions, forged in the theft of Indigenous lands and captive labors, that continue to conscript students and their families, teachers and researchers, administrators and service contractors, bankers and speculators, and corporate managers and policy wonks in processes of growth and expansion. As la paperson puts it, "universities are land-grabbing, land-transmogrifying, land-capitalizing machines." They are "gigantic machines that are attached to other machines: war machines, media machines, governmental and nongovernmental policy machines."[55] All of this was clear to Harding and his comrades in 1970, or at least enough so that the IBW had to be forged in flight.[56] In the intervening half century, conditions have only gotten worse.

The university, la paperson writes, is a "world-*making*" institution, nowadays an amalgamation of three distinct "*worlding* formations."[57] Rooted in the logic of accumulation, "first worlding universities are machinery commissioned to actualize imperialist dreams of a settled world." Here we identify the "academic-industrial complex: 'research-ones' preeminently, but also commercial

universities and any other corporate academic enterprise that, regardless of its
formal and thematic diversity, is characterized by an ultimate commitment to
brand expansion and accumulation of patent, publication, and prestige." There
is also a "second" worlding formation, born of a "desire to humanize" and liberate, at least in the mold of Enlightenment liberalism. This formation, often
reflected in liberal arts colleges, "may indeed offer meaningful challenges to the
academic-industrial complex, and could be said to be a democratic and partic-
ipatory academy that seeks to challenge and provoke the critical consciousness
of its students toward self-actualization." But this second worlding formation is
defined by the "pursuit of questions of art, humanities, and a libertarian mode
of critical thinking" that "displaces the possibility of sustained, radical critique
and thereby remains circumscribed 'within the ivory tower.'"[58]

The mode of the second university is at least part of what we are engaged in
here, in our interpretation and application of King. This is the work of critical
theory, of the deconstruction of systems of power and oppression. Such critical
work is essential work. But all too frequently, critique remains only discursively
or ideologically radical. Its lessons carry a "hidden curriculum" that "reflects
the material conditions of higher education—fees, degrees, expertise, and the
presumed emancipatory possibilities of the mind." In other words, critique
tends to depend upon and thus "reinscribe academic accumulation." When we
wax nostalgic about the world-expanding possibilities of a liberal arts education, la paperson says, we are "rarely talking about a university that rematriates
land, that disciplines scholar-warriors rather than 'liberating' its students, that
repurposes the industrial machinery, that supports insurrectionary national-
isms as problematic antidotes to imperialist nationalism, that acts upon financial systems rather than just critiquing them, that helps in the accumulation of
third world power rather than simply disavowing first world power, that is a
school-to-community pipeline, not a community-to-school pipeline."[59]

As we consider the afterlives of King's critique, we must question where this
critique lives, how it lives, how it could be made to live and learn and grow in
ways that are consistent with the fullness of King's activist work and movement
legacy. As an exercise in critical theory, it can be nurtured in the compromised
space of the second university, informed by an external world that holds it in
possession. But, in the legacy of King—and of Harding—it cannot in good
faith be sequestered in the pages of an academic book or in the memory of a
liberal arts college alumna who loved her seminar on Black history but who
went on to work in sales and still owes tens of thousands of dollars on her student loans.

Harding, for his part, rejected the imperialism of the first university and disavowed the liberal escapism of the second. He sought to reorient Black study and scholarship around the principle of "community in struggle." In this, his vision aligns with what la paperson refers to as the university's "third worlding" formation. Implicit in this phrasing are connections with the Third World Liberation Front, including the watershed battle over Black studies at San Francisco State University in 1968, and the larger legacy of the Bandung Conference of 1955 and the anti-colonial movements of the Global South. The "third world" locution is not accidental. Within the modern university are "decolonial riders," "by-products," pieces of "colonialist scrap" who "desire against the assemblage" that made them.[60] Here the work is "interdisciplinary, transnational, yet vocational," and very much in the way that Harding imagined.[61] It all goes on in the university's "underground," as Harney and Moten would say, in the "downlow lowdown maroon community of the university," in the *undercommons of enlightenment*, where the work gets done, where the work gets subverted, where the revolution is still black, still strong."[62]

Whether we are referring to Harding and his IBW comrades or those involved in contemporary debates over "Black study," the idea is to nurture prophetic assemblages of inquiry and action that go well beyond academic critique, well beyond what Harding called the "ponderous uncertainties of 'the scholarly community.'"[63] It is not clear that King's critique of racial capitalism is most at home in the university, even in its undercommons. This is why the case of the IBW—and perhaps the more speculative, untested idea of the Black university, which would necessarily bear fewer traces of the colonial university's three formations—remains instructive.

The IBW practiced a form of "collective scholarship" as a deliberate counter to capitalism's technologies of partition and individuation, which in our neoliberal moment are so frequently replicated in the disciplinary wall building and credentialing processes of the professionalized academy. As Harding put it, "in the same way that we break beyond false boundaries of Western colonialism, attempting to recreate our essential Pan-African unity, expressing our solidarity with the larger pro-human struggles, so too our truth demands that we reject the artificial barriers of the academic disciplines to seek the human unity which underlies the experience of our people."[64] Surely this was intended to help safeguard against narrow knowledge production and the commodification of scholarship and credentialed expertise that could be packaged and neatly sold into the technocratic calculus. But more to the point, such "collective scholarship" signals a mode of speculative togetherness and movement building that is less derivative of the university, less well defined by subversive flight into its netherworlds, less interested in "stealing what one can." It is more an act of building than of taking.

Perhaps we can come at the point via IBW lecturer James Boggs. During his 1974 visit to the IBW in Atlanta, Boggs spoke of race and class, indeed of racial capitalism, and of the need to battle contradictions in struggle. "The eruption of the black movement," he said, "exposed the historical connection between racism and capitalism and made it clear that it was not possible to get rid of racism in this country without getting rid of American capitalism any more than it was possible to carry on a struggle to reform the South without carrying on a struggle to change this entire nation." Any struggle, he continued, "may start out with the aim of resolving one contradiction. But in the course of the struggle, if the contradiction which it sets out to negate is fundamental enough, the main contradiction may change; it may become enlarged or expanded. Struggle is social practice and when you engage in social practice, you gain new insights. You find out that there was much more involved than you had originally perceived to be the case when you began your struggle." In this way, "you are faced with the need to raise your level of understanding, your level of conceptual knowledge. If you do not raise your level of understanding as the struggle expands and develops, then what began as a progressive struggle can turn into its opposite."[65]

What Boggs is describing is the critique of racial capitalism born and bred in the movement of a people. This aligns with the story we have sought to tell of King—a figure who was both *in* and *of* what Boggs calls "social practice," who battled contradictions in solidarity with his people, who in the process was made to see other contradictions, to elevate his consciousness, to speak and write about his findings, and to keep learning and growing and building. It is this "social practice" that scholarly institutions must attach themselves to if they are to stay true to the spirit of King's critique. If the university is ill suited for this task, as Harding seems to have concluded a half-century ago, then perhaps we must continue seeking institutional girders elsewhere, perhaps in those "black institutions" that are "yet to be born."

"To Speak Now of Building . . ."

To be sure, King's critique is at home in what contemporary theorists call Black study. "We are committed," Moten says, "to the idea that study is what you do with other people. It's talking and walking around with other people, working, dancing, suffering, some irreducible convergence of all three, held under the name of speculative practice. The notion of a rehearsal—being in a kind of workshop, playing in a band, in a jam session, or old men sitting on a porch, or people working together in a factory—there are these various modes of activity. The point of calling it 'study' is to mark that the incessant and irreversible intellectuality of these activities is already present."[66] It is truly striking how well this formulation of Black study resonates with King's vision of life and labor in the beloved community, in that rising tumult of aspiring mutuality, necessarily speculative, with one foot planted in and another stepping out beyond the constraints of the racial capitalist order. King relished the thought of ordinary people taking the time to a read a book and engage their neighbors in conversation about its subject matter. And, most crucially and most scandalously, he imagined people *getting paid for doing this*. Or, if we prefer a less wage-centered formulation, *materially sustained for doing this*. The point is that this kind of Black study, what Moten goes on to call "a sort of sociality," demonstrates its worthlessness as a fuel for the engines of commerce and indicates very clearly that new engines, productive forces that can run on sociality as a more sustainable biofuel, must be built.[67]

One overarching objective of this book has been to consider how King wrestled with the suffocating constraints of the racial capitalist machine. The great dreamer knew that we can't just dream up the revolution of values. As Harding put it, King "was wise enough to know that you can't get at values just by saying you're going to get at values. You've also got to get at the structures that support the values."[68] Black study as an afterlife of King's critique requires not only ideological and epistemic work, but also a fully embodied confrontation with the technologies of racial capitalism: its mechanisms, its material circuits, its institutions that enable and sustain its reproduction. The marginal spaces of the modern university are but one case study. And one key lesson from this case is that we must look beyond the "'representational' work of knowledge production that we associate with the university" in order to also confront "the steam and pistons, the waterworks, the groundworks, the investments, the institutional-governmental-capitalistic rhizomatics of the university."[69]

Contemporary notions of a fugitive Black study that is "in but not of" the university reflect both a certain optimism about the richness of the transgressive work always already thriving in the undercommons, but also a certain pessimism about institutional change. Robin D. G. Kelley points out how this scholarly fugitivity bears relation to IBW comrade Walter Rodney's notion of the "guerilla intellectual." But "unlike Rodney's guerrilla intellectuals," Kelley says, "Harney and Moten's guerrillas are not preparing to strike, planning to seize power, contesting the university (or the state; the difference isn't always clear)—at least not on the terms they have set. To do so would be to recognize the university and its legitimacy and to be invested in its regimes of professionalization."[70] The concern, as Harney puts it, is that "by making a request to authority one is already implicating oneself."[71] But if the traditionally recognized university and its regimes of professionalization hurdle toward a legitimacy crisis as neoliberal inequality and Black suffering carry forth, perhaps questions of abolitionism and flight take on a new salience. The limitations of making a claim on authority are real. But beyond practices of sneaking in and stealing what one can, the prospect of simply abandoning these institutional spaces is becoming both more viable and more imperative.

For decades the neoliberal imagination has been consumed by the specter of "dark times." Things have become so bleak, so despairing that, to paraphrase Wendy Brown, we are unsure if it is just the times that are dark or the world itself.[72] Part of the value in revisiting the era of King and Harding, of sympathizing with the collective struggles of the Black radical tradition, is that it helps to situate the scholarly fugitivity of today's neoliberal pessimism in historical perspective. Not unlike the most sobering critics today, King and Harding grasped the power of the possessive hold, the ways in which our extant organizations— and the state, the market, the antiblackness that possess them—are set up to reproduce themselves. King and Harding were, like we are, thoroughly discontented with all of this. But their era reflected a spirit of collective worldmaking that put the times in their place, as moments in history. King was able to cast his era's "deep rumbling of discontent" as the "thunder of disinherited masses rising from dungeons of oppression to the bright hills of freedom."[73] The powerful and exploitative profiteers "resent our discontent," he said, because they "resent our organizing."[74] It is this worldmaking spirit—born of critique, necessarily collective in nature—that led King's scholarly heirs to take flight even of the undercommons and to strike out into the open, to join together in bold and disciplined efforts to build, indeed to institute, the Black world.

Let us not forget that King warned about integrating into a burning house.[75] Does Black study in the tradition of King call for some kind of reinvestment in established universities and their "institutional-governmental-capitalistic rhizomatics"? Or are we called to look for a fire exit and turn our attention to building up the likes of the Highlander Center and the Institute of the Black World? Harding put the question this way: "What institutions must be discarded now in order that they may be more fully prepared to break the circle of white power? What chances and risks must we take in our own time in order to help them towards better positions for their own overcoming movement?" These are the kinds of questions—at once wildly visionary yet life-directing and immediately pragmatic—that present themselves in the afterlives of King's critique. For ultimately, King spoke of a "black revolution," one that "reveals systemic rather than superficial flaws and suggests that radical reconstruction of society itself is the real issue to be faced."[76] It remains frightful and uncertain work, but such is the struggle to bridge the decline of one world and the eruption of another.

By the time King's life gave way to its afterlives, frightfulness and uncertainty had become prominent themes for him.[77] He was deep into the second phase of his struggle. Reform had given way to revolution, and he repeatedly reminded himself and his audiences that so much of the modern world as we have come to know it had to be forsaken, including material support for movement work to rebuild that very world. To commit to addressing systemic rather than superficial flaws "may mean the death of your bridge to the White House," he said to SCLC colleagues in his last year. "It may mean the death of a foundation grant. It may cut your budget down a little."[78] But this is precisely the biting edge of the critique, and by no means does it signal the death of the work. The movement endures. Our efforts to reconstruct King's critical theory of capitalist society have led us to interpret and translate his ideas, to fill in gaps and occasionally move beyond his words and context. But we have uncovered a few threads—a distinctive dialectical mode of inquiry, an analysis of how human beings are held in relation to one another and differentially valued under capitalism, a sense that capitalist society requires and reproduces violent enforcement of racial formations and inequalities, on both domestic and international stages. We have homed in on King's sense that, as he put it in his last year, "racism, economic exploitation and militarism are all tied together," that "you can't really get rid of one without getting rid of the others."[79] King's critique belongs to the tradition that shaped it, that carried on after his death, and that continues to reverberate within today's insurgent Black movements.

Chapter One. "The Trouble Is . . ."

1. For these quotations from King as well as a recollection of the events that evening, see Belafonte and Shnayerson, *My Song*, 326–328.

2. Kelley, "Introduction," 5; Khan-Cullors and bandele, *When They Call You a Terrorist*, 86–88.

3. See, for example, West, *Radical King*; Laurent, *King and the Other America*; Honey, *To the Promised Land*; Dorrien, *Breaking White Supremacy*; Le Blanc, "Martin Luther King."

4. For his own account of his reading of Marx's *Capital* in 1949, see King, *Stride toward Freedom*, 78.

5. King, *Where Do We Go from Here?*, 88.

6. Robinson, *Black Marxism*, 2.

7. In a later book, *Black Movements in America*, Robinson featured King as an exemplary religious figure in a broadly Black radical tradition, though he did not consider King's economic analysis.

8. In a major new edited volume on King's political philosophy, for example, the only essay dedicated to an analysis of King's economic thinking—Tommie Shelby's "Prisons of the Forgotten"—is better understood as a contribution in normative moral philosophy.

9. Relevant works include: Garrow, *Bearing the Cross*; Honey, *Going Down Jericho Road*; T. Jackson, *From Civil Rights to Human Rights*; Honey, *To the Promised Land*.

10. See Phillips, "In the latest JFK files." On King's alleged Marxism, see also Fairclough, "Was Martin Luther King a Marxist?" To date, the most thoughtful treatment of King's affinities with Marxist theory is Laurent, *King and the Other America*.

11. Fraser and Jaeggi, *Capitalism*.

12. Kelley, "Introduction," 7.

13. See the excerpts of Marx's writings collected in "Marx on Slavery and the U.S. Civil War."

14. Marx, *Capital,* vol. 1, chap. 26.

15. Mbembe, *Critique of Black Reason*, 23.

16. Cox, *Capitalism as a System*, 213–214.

17. Smallwood, "What Slavery Tells Us about Marx," 82.

18. King, "Retail, Wholesale," 61.

19. Fraser, "Behind Marx's Hidden Abode," 56–57.

20. Dawson, "Hidden in Plain Sight," 147–148. Nancy Fraser, too, has gone on to embrace this argument about the centrality of racial expropriation in the reproduction of capitalist society. See Fraser and Jaeggi, *Capitalism*, 39–47, 101–108.

21. Melamed, "Racial Capitalism," 77. See also Melamed, *Represent and Destroy*.

22. King, "Freedom's Crisis"; Jackson, *From Civil Rights to Human Rights*, 38, 250–251.

23. Reed, "Introduction to Oliver C. Cox," xiii.

24. Clarno, *Neoliberal Apartheid*, 10; Wang, *Carceral Capitalism*, 88.

25. Dawson, "Hidden in Plain Sight," 151.

26. Akuno and Nangwaya, *Jackson Rising*, 9.

27. King, "Speech at SCLC Staff Retreat" [1966], 7, 8. See also King, "Other America" [1968].

28. Malcolm X, "Harlem 'Hate-Gang' Scare," 69.

29. King did say rather starkly to the SCLC staff in 1967 that "racism, economic exploitation and militarism are all tied together," that "you can't really get rid of one without getting rid of the others" ("Speech at SCLC Staff Retreat" [1967]). For a helpful survey of the twentieth-century Black Left in America, see Dawson, *Blacks In and Out of the Left*.

30. See Akuno and Nangwaya, *Jackson Rising*; Kelley, "Coates and West in Jackson"; Moskowitz, "Meet the Radical Workers' Cooperative."

31. Robinson, *Black Marxism*, xxx–xxxi.

32. A. Gordon, preface to *Anthropology of Marxism*, x–xi.

33. Roediger, *Class, Race, and Marxism*, 9–10.

34. See, for example, Robinson and Morse, "Capitalism, Marxism, and the Black Radical Tradition "; Scott, "On the Very Idea of the Black Radical Tradition"; Cunningham, "A Queer Pier"; Roberts, "Theorizing Freedom"; Meyerson, "Rethinking Black Marxism."

35. On Coretta Scott King's activism in the '70s, '80s, and '90s, see Theoharis, "'I am not a symbol,'" and Scott King, *My Life, My Love, My Legacy*. For an account of the strategy of "thinking with King beyond King," see Threadcraft and Terry, "Gender Trouble."

36. Robinson, *Black Marxism*, 168.

37. Robinson, *Black Marxism*, 168.

38. Robinson, *Terms of Order*.

39. Robinson, *Terms of Order*, 1.

40. White, *Challenge of Blackness*.

41. Robinson, *Black Marxism*, xxxii.

42. King, "Beyond Vietnam," 215.

Chapter Two. "The Other America"

1. King, "Other America" [1968], 159.

2. Tully, *Public Philosophy*; Marx, "Letter to Arnold Ruge," 2.

3. Tully, *Public Philosophy*, 28–29.

4. Dawson, "Future of Black Politics." Note also the parallels with Du Bois, who insisted that "criticism is the soul of democracy and the safeguard of modern society" (*Souls of Black Folk*, 36). On King's appreciation of Du Bois—whom he regarded not only as a "teacher" to those who read him but also as a preeminent theorist of "divine dissatisfaction"—see King, "Honoring Dr. Du Bois."

5. Lloyd, *Black Natural Law*, x.

6. Robinson, *Black Marxism*, 168.

7. See King, "Other America" [1967].

8. Harrington, *Other America*; National Advisory Commission on Civil Disorders, *Kerner Report*, 1.

9. King, "Other America" [1968], 156.

10. Baldwin, *Voice of Conscience*, 45. For a discussion of King's involvement in the labor movement, see Honey, *Going Down Jericho Road* and *To the Promised Land*; and King's writings collected in Honey, ed., *"All Labor Has Dignity."*

11. Baker, *Betrayal*, 7. On his connection with the poor and working classes, King "was nothing if not consistent," notes the historian Michael Honey. "Going back to his days in graduate school, he had spoken of his strong concern for the poor based on his Social Gospel theology. He had championed 'we, the dispossessed' in Montgomery. He had constantly spoken and written about and organized around issues confronting poor and working-class people. He had indicted the Vietnam War as a crime that used poor people as cannon fodder and destroyed resources that should have gone to ending their poverty" (*To the Promised Land*, 122). As Sylvie Laurent notes, King's roots in the Black social gospel ensured that he "was immersed in a spiritual framework which has its own tradition of care and dedication to the poor" (*King and the Other America*, 73). For further discussion of King's sensitivity to the poor, developed very early on, see Baldwin, *There is a Balm in Gilead*, 123; Honey, *To the Promised Land*, 19; and Dorrien, *Breaking White Supremacy*, 18-19.

12. See Drezner, *Ideas Industry*.

13. Baker, *Betrayal*, vi.

14. Spence, *Knocking the Hustle*, 111. Despite this book's many strengths, its treatment of King is strikingly disingenuous, if not altogether nonsensical. Spence commits a performative contradiction of sorts, offering, as he does, essentially an intellectual critique of intellectualism. And in treating King almost exclusively as a rhetorician, a master of "prophetic utterance," Spence misses entirely both the rich substance of King's social criticism and, most remarkably, King's demonstrable record of driving people to do precisely the sort of hard political work that Spence calls for.

15. King, "'Beyond Condemnation,'" 199.

16. Baker, *Betrayal*, 22.

17. Reed, *Class Notes*.

18. See Branch, *Parting the Waters*, 93–110 passim; and Dorrien, *Breaking White Supremacy*, 271, 276–287.

19. See Ansbro, *Martin Luther King, Jr.*, 122.

20. See King, "Letter from Birmingham City Jail," 289–302.

21. King, *Stride toward Freedom*, 89.

22. King, *Strength to Love*, 1.

23. See King, *Stride Toward Freedom*, 83–84. See also King, "My Pilgrimage to Non-violence," 475–477. "I read Marx as I read all of the influential historical thinkers—from a dialectical point of view, combining a partial 'yes' and a partial 'no.' In so far as Marx posited a metaphysical materialism, an ethical relativism, and a strangulating totalitarianism, I responded with an unambiguous 'no'; but in so far as he pointed to weaknesses of traditional capitalism, contributed to the growth of a definite self-consciousness in the masses, and challenged the social conscience of the Christian churches, I responded with a definite 'yes.' My reading of Marx also convinced me that truth is found neither in Marxism nor in traditional capitalism. Each represents a partial truth. Historically capitalism failed to see the truth in collective enterprise, and Marxism failed to see the truth in individual enterprise. Nineteenth century capitalism failed to see that life is social and Marxism failed and still fails to see that life is individual and personal. The Kingdom of God is neither the thesis of individual enterprise nor the antithesis of collective enterprise, but a synthesis which reconciles the truths of both."

24. S. Ferguson, "The Philosopher King," 103.

25. S. Ferguson, "The Philosopher King," 103, citing King's final address to the SCLC: "For years . . . I have labored with the idea of reforming the existing institutions of the society. A little change here, a little change thee. Now I feel quite differently. I think you've got to have a reconstruction of the entire society, a revolution of values."

26. James, *Notes on Dialectics*, 91–92.

27. Consider, for example, King's 1965 reflections on poverty, in which he calls for a "mental and spiritual re-evaluation—a change of focus which will enable us to see that the things which seem most real and powerful are indeed now unreal and have come under the sentence of death." This is an unmistakably dialectical assertion. The moment of negativity, the presumption of the irrationality and therefore untruth of extant reality, is borne along by a commitment to ongoing historical movement toward rational reconciliation. King continues: "We will not build a peaceful world by following a negative path . . . we must fix our visions not merely on the negative expulsion of war, but upon the positive affirmation of peace" ("Octopus of Poverty," 119).

28. See James, *Notes on Dialectics*, 29, and, for a fuller interpretive commentary, Douglas, *In the Spirit of Critique*, 100–107.

29. On King's encounter with James, see James, "A Visit with Martin Luther King," and King, "To C. L. R. James."

30. King, "Other America" [1968], 160. Though we do not pursue the comparison here, it might be worth noting that the trope of "despair" has a certain salience in post-Hegelian critical theory, including its Black radical iterations. See, for example, the discussion of Frantz Fanon in Marasco, *Highway of Despair*.

31. King, "Other America" [1968], 159.

32. King, *Stride toward Freedom*, 31.

33. These arguments about the implicit rationalism and narrative plot structure of the modern dialectical tradition are developed in much greater detail, albeit without discussion of King, in Douglas, *In the Spirit of Critique*. For a rich treatment of the reconciliatory "mode of emplotment" in the dialectical and historical theory of C. L. R. James, see Scott, *Conscripts of Modernity*, and for a critique of the European cultural imperialist dimensions of the Hegelian dialectical tradition, see Ciccariello-Maher, *Decolonizing Dialectics*. It is important to acknowledge, too, that King's mobilization of this aspect of the dialectical tradition can be said to reinforce troublesome denials of agency, including, for example, King's patriarchal denial of Rosa Parks' agency in the Montgomery struggle. On this point, see Threadcraft and Terry, "Gender Trouble."

34. Jameson, "Persistencies of the Dialectic," 366. See also Jameson, *Valences of the Dialectic*.

35. Burrow, *God and Human Dignity*, 190.

36. Baldwin, *Voice of Conscience*, 81.

37. Lloyd, *Black Natural Law*, 117, emphasis added.

38. Lloyd, *Black Natural Law*, 117. On "negative theology," see also Lloyd's commentary on how the Black natural law tradition challenges the terms of European humanism. Following Sylvia Wynter—and, we might add, in the vein of Frantz Fanon's earlier challenge to the idea of "European man"—Lloyd argues for a "rejection of the concept of man, burdened with its particularly white, European, and masculine associations, and for the development of a new concept of the human . . . a concept of the human [that is] essentially defined by what it is not, marking what is in the world but never fully captured by it" (*Black Natural Law*, xi; see also Wynter, "Unsettling the Coloniality"; Fanon, *Black Skin, White Masks*; Fanon, *Wretched of the Earth*.)

39. King, "Letter from Birmingham City Jail," 295.

40. Baker, *Betrayal*, 38.

41. Lloyd, *Black Natural Law*, x, xii.

42. Marx and Engels, *German Ideology*, 67.

43. Geuss, *Philosophy and Real Politics*, 52.

44. King, "Other America" [1968], 162–164.

45. See Roediger, *Wages of Whiteness*; Du Bois, *Black Reconstruction in America*, 700. See also King, "Honoring Dr. Du Bois." Though he did not specifically mention Du Bois's idea that white people in the United States reap a sort of unearned psychological benefit or "wage" simply by virtue of their whiteness, King certainly described Du Bois very explicitly as a pioneer in the field of ideology critique. Du Bois was a "teacher" who challenged the "poisonous fog of lies," the "twisted logic," the "army of white propagandists—the myth-makers of Negro history," and who "restored to light the most luminous achievement[s] of the Reconstruction," including "free public education . . . not only for the benefit of the Negro" but also "poor whites," and "the Negroes' capacity to govern and fitness to build a finer nation in a creative relationship with poor whites" (113–117).

46. "Fetish, n. 1b." OED Online. December 2020. Oxford University Press. https://www-oed-com.ezproxy.auctr.edu/view/Entry/69611?rskey=s7gHBp&result=1 (accessed January 13, 2021).

47. Marx, *Capital*, 1:165–166, emphasis added.

48. Harvey, *Companion to Marx's* Capital, 41.

49. Roberts, *Marx's Inferno*, 85.

50. See, for example, King, *Where Do We Go from Here?*, 196.

51. Consider Frank Wilderson's claim that "violence against black people is ontological and gratuitous as opposed to merely ideological and contingent" ("Gramsci's Black Marx," 229). King would agree, though he clearly historicized racial formations in ways that render his thought incompatible with the grander claims of the contemporary Afropessimist school.

52. Lloyd, *Black Natural Law*, xiv.

53. Marx, *Capital*, 1:167–168.

54. Lloyd, *Black Natural Law*, 101.

55. King, "Where Do We Go from Here?," 250.

56. Roberts, *Marx's Inferno*, 102.

57. Roberts, *Marx's Inferno*, 96.

58. King, "Letter from Birmingham City Jail," 292.

59. Baldwin, *Voice of Conscience*, 97.

60. This phrase, or some variation of it, enjoys a long lineage among critical and radical thinkers in the modern West and beyond; we highlight one popularization of it, well known in certain circles, by Kwame Nkrumah, King's contemporary and decolonial comrade. See Nkrumah, *Consciencism*, 78.

61. Dawson, "Future of Black Politics"; Roberts, *Marx's Inferno*, 99.

62. Edwards, foreword, *Terms of Order*, xviii–xix.

63. Edwards, foreword, *Terms of Order*, xviii; see also A. Gordon, preface to *Anthropology of Marxism*, xi.

64. King, "Other America" [1968], 166.

65. King, "Notecards on Books of the Old Testament," 165, emphasis added.

66. Geuss, *Politics and the Imagination*, 42.

Chapter Three. "Something Is Wrong with Capitalism"

1. King, "Beyond Vietnam," 214.

2. References to a "second phase" abound in the correspondences, public and private addresses, and published writings of King's later years. See, for example, King's remarks to colleagues at the 1966 Southern Christian Leadership Conference: "even though we gained legislative and judicial victories during this period [the decade following the 1955 Montgomery bus boycott] . . . we must admit it: the changes that came about during this period were at best surface changes, they were not really substantive

changes" ("Speech at SCLC Staff Retreat" [1966], 6). See also King, "New Sense of Direction," 6.

3. Scholarly work aside, consider two popular pieces published recently, on the occasion of King's birthday: Sustar, "The Evolution of Dr. King," and Dreier, "Martin Luther King Was A Democratic Socialist."

4. See Marx, *Capital,* 1:255–256: "Capital is money, capital is commodities. In truth, however, value is here the subject of a process in which while constantly assuming the form in turn of money and commodities, it changes its own magnitude, throws off surplus-value from itself. . . . Money therefore forms the starting point and the conclusion of every valorization process. . . . Value therefore now becomes *value in process,* money in process, and, as such, capital." See also Marx, *Capital,* 2:211. Note that the Penguin translation has it as "value in process," though our analysis draws on the work of Harvey, who, in *The Limits to Capital* and elsewhere, vivifies this reading of capital as "value in motion."

5. See Marx, *Capital,* 1:149.

6. See King, "Man Who was a Fool," 73: "In a real sense all life is inter-related. All men are caught in an inescapable network of mutuality, tied in a single garment of destiny. Whatever affects one directly, affects all indirectly. I can never be what I ought to be until you are what you ought to be, and you can never be what you ought to be until I am what I ought to be. . . . This is the inter-related structure of reality."

7. Fraser and Jaeggi, *Capitalism,* 40–42.

8. See King, *Stride Toward Freedom,* 78.

9. King, "Beyond Vietnam: A Time to Break Silence," 214.

10. Heideman and Birch, "Trouble with Anti-Antiracism."

11. For a discussion of the Montgomery city contract with the Chicago-based National City Lines, including an account of how, as that private firm lost money, it put further pressure on the city, see Garrow, *Bearing the Cross,* 26–28, 52; and Jackson, *Becoming King,* 131–132.

12. See Hall, "Long Civil Rights Movement"; G. Gilmore, *Defying Dixie*; Ezra, *Economic Civil Rights Movement.* See also King's appreciation of Reinhold Niebuhr's Depression-era writings on the boycott as a weapon in the struggle against racial discrimination (*Where Do We Go from Here?,* 151).

13. Cited in Garrow, *Bearing the Cross,* 43.

14. Laurent, *King and the Other America,* 72–73. See also Gary Dorrien's review of King's intellectual influences, both within the Black church and in formal schooling, and how readers of King have at times been misled, partly owing to King's own account of his intellectual development (*Breaking White Supremacy,* 260–281).

15. "I studied philosophy and theology at Boston University under Edgar S. Brightman and L. Harold DeWolf. . . . It was mainly under these teachers that I studied Personalistic philosophy—the theory that the clue to the meaning of ultimate reality is found in personality. This personal idealism remains today my basic philosophical position." (King, *Autobiography,* 31).

16. King, "Beyond Vietnam," 214.

17. King, *Autobiography*, 31.

18. Williams and Bengtsson, "Personalism."

19. "Alienation is a form of living death," King said in 1967. "It is the acid of despair that dissolves society" (*Trumpet of Conscience*, 44). King's references to alienation tend not to reflect the traditional Marxist concern about estranged labor, but rather a concern with social estrangement and the psychology of racism and consumerism. There is no evidence that King ever read Marx's early and more "humanist" writings. In late 1949, King read *Capital* and *The Communist Manifesto*. King admired Erich Fromm, though apparently he did not read Fromm's groundbreaking 1961 study, *Marx's Concept of Man*, which, in effect, introduced the Western world to Marx's humanistic writings. This is yet another sign of how King's critique of political economy gestured beyond the conceptual tools of European radicalism; as we discuss below, King's emphasis on consumerism and the circulation of consumer goods through unequal social relations speaks presciently to the lived realities of a postproduction neoliberal economy. See, for example, King, "Along this Way," where he refers simply to "the legion of damned in our economic army," a condition in which "the Negro in America is an impoverished alien in an affluent society" (quoted in Laurent, *King and the Other America*, 121).

20. King, "Three Dimensions of a Complete Life," 43.

21. Dorrien, *Breaking White Supremacy*, 304–305, 309.

22. For a recent commentary on King's subjection to anticommunist hysteria, see Honey, *To the Promised Land*.

23. On King's evolving disavowal of Marx and Marxism, in addition to recent work by Laurent, Honey, and Dorrien, see Fairclough, "Was Martin Luther King a Marxist?," 117–125.

24. Berdyaev, "Marx and Personalism."

25. J. Pius Barbour, quoted in Garrow, *Bearing the Cross*, 43; King, "Speech at SCLC Staff Retreat" [1966], 20.

26. Watson, "Letter to King," 156–157.

27. Robinson, *Black Marxism*, 168–169.

28. See Sokol, *There Goes My Everything*, 93–94; T. F. Jackson, *From Civil Rights to Human Rights*, 279; Honey's introduction to King's "To the Mountaintop," 181. (Emphasis added.)

29. For King's famous reference to "shallow things," see, "Drum Major Instinct," 264.

30. Melamed, "Racial Capitalism," 78. See also the discussion of "expropriation" and the violence of its "colonial logic" in Dawson, "Hidden in Plain Sight," and Fraser, "Expropriation and Exploitation."

31. Melamed, "Racial Capitalism," 78.

32. R. Gilmore, "Race and Globalization," 261, emphasis added.

33. King, "Speech at SCLC Staff Retreat" [1966], 7, 8. See also Andy Clarno's account of a "necropolitics" that, he argues, is characteristic of racial capitalism: "capitalism

consistently operates through racial projects that assign differential value to human life and labor. Yet racism cannot be reduced to an effect of capitalism; rather, processes of racial formation are relatively autonomous from and constitutive of capital accumulation. While white supremacy may intensify exploitation by devaluing Black labor, it can also generate 'necropolitical' projects that equate the security of the white population with the elimination of Black, indigenous, or other devalued populations" (*Neoliberal Apartheid*, 9).

34. See Marx's preface to *Contribution to the Critique of Political Economy*. For an account of how this "big-picture" Marxist development narrative—the emphasis on the expansion of social and productive capacity—figures in the work of Walter Rodney, another exemplary theorist of what we might call the Black radical tradition, see Douglas, "'Brutal Dialectics.'"

35. King, "Will Capitalism Survive," 104.

36. See, for example, King's account of the "problem bequeathed to us by the accelerated progress of science. As machines replace men, we must again question whether the depth of our social thinking matches the growth of technological creativity. We cannot create machines which revolutionize industry unless we simultaneously create ideas commensurate with social and economic reorganization, which harnesses the power of such machines for the benefit of man" ("Thirteenth Convention," 51).

37. On the theory of "underdevelopment," see Rodney, *How Europe Underdeveloped Africa*, and Marable, *How Capitalism Underdeveloped Black America*. King's position here is quite consistent with the summary findings of the Kerner Commission: "What white Americans have never fully understood—but what the Negro can never forget—is that white society is deeply implicated in the ghetto. White institutions created it, white institutions maintain it, and white society condones it" (National Advisory Commission on Civil Disorders, *Kerner Report*, 2).

38. King, "Freedom's Crisis," 288–292. "We have yet to confront and solve the international problems created by our wealth in a world still largely hungry and miserable. But more immediate and pressing is the domestic existence of poverty. It is an anachronism in the second half of the 20th century. Only the neglect to plan intelligently and adequately and the unwillingness genuinely to embrace economic justice enable it to persist." Or, "the question on the agenda must read: why should there be hunger and privation in any land, in any city, at any table, when man has the resources and the scientific know-how to provide all mankind with basic necessities of life" (King, *Where Do We Go from Here?*, 187). It is also worth noting King's observations about how social awareness moves, and does not move, across racial capitalism's spatial boundaries: "while so many white Americans are unaware of conditions inside the ghetto, there are very few ghetto dwellers who are unaware of the life outside. . . . It is not only poverty that torments the Negro; it is poverty amid plenty. It is a misery generated by the gulf between the affluence he sees in the mass media and the deprivation he experiences in his everyday life" (*Where Do We Go from Here?*, 119). Compare James Ralph's observation: "throughout much of American history blacks were exploited, beaten, and oppressed

while most Americans and people around the world went about their daily affairs barely aware of the situation. Indeed, racial segregation and oppression isolated blacks from the American mainstream, making their wretched conditions invisible" (*Northern Protest*). See also Finley et al., *Chicago Freedom Movement*.

39. King, "Freedom's Crisis," emphasis added. See also Jackson, *From Civil Rights to Human Rights*, 250–251.

40. Garrow, *Bearing the Cross*, 430.

41. King, "Southern Christian Leadership Conference," 188. See also Laurent, *King and the Other America*, 222–224. This conception of "internal colonialism" has a long history in Black radical thought, and King can be described as latecomer. See, for example, Joshua Bloom and Waldo E. Martin's discussion of the use of the term among members of the Revolutionary Action Movement in the mid-1960s and, later, the Black Panther Party, in *Black against Empire*. For a critique of the 1960s-era application of the thesis as it applies to an understanding of the exploitative nature of racial capitalism, see Taylor, *From #BlackLivesMatter to Black Liberation*, 196–197.

42. Melamed, "Racial Capitalism," 78.

43. Melamed, "Racial Capitalism," 78–79.

44. Marx, "Theories of Surplus Value."

45. Harvey, *Limits to Capital*, 192.

46. Marx, *Capital*, 3:351.

47. See Jackson, *From Civil Rights to Human Rights*, chap. 5, for a helpful discussion of how, by 1962, King's thinking was profoundly affected by concerns about deindustrialization, ghettoization, and structural joblessness.

48. King, "Thirteenth Convention," 51.

49. See, for example, the reference to "nobodiness" in King, "Letter from Birmingham City Jail," 289–302.

50. Denning, "Wageless Life."

51. See Endnotes Collective, "Misery and Debt," 30n15. See also Chen, "Limit Point": "The rise of the anti-black U.S. carceral state from the 1970s onward exemplifies rituals of state and civilian violence which enforce the racialization of wageless life, and the racial ascription of wagelessness. From the point of view of capital, 'race' is renewed not only through persistent racialized wage differentials, or the kind of occupational segregation posited by earlier 'split labor market' theories of race, but through the racialization of unwaged surplus or superfluous populations from Khartoum to the slums of Cairo" (217). See also Kali Akuno's account of how "Black disposability," which he fears will have a "genocidal effect" on the Black working class if left unchallenged, is the driving point of emphasis for the exemplary justice struggles underway in Jackson, Mississippi (Akuno and Nangwaya, *Jackson Rising*, 8–9).

52. King, *Where Do We Go from Here?*, 172.

53. Melamed, "Racial Capitalism," 77. Also relevant here is the theory of "accumulation by dispossession," which accounts for how neoliberal growth crises have shifted the pursuit of profit away from expanded reproduction and toward various modes of

privatization of public assets (see Harvey, *New Imperialism* and Harvey, *Seventeen Contradictions*). See also Chakravartty and da Silva, "Accumulation, Dispossession, and Debt," for a cogent discussion of dispossession through predatory finance and racialized debt incumbency.

54. Cited in Garrow, *Bearing the Cross*, 574.

55. Cited in Garrow, *Bearing the Cross*, 579, 582.

56. Consider, for example, King's frequent reference to the Biblical parable of Dives and Lazarus, which was a persistent set piece for him, from his early days pastoring at Dexter Avenue Baptist Church in Montgomery to his final Sunday sermon at the National Cathedral. Even in that final Sunday sermon, in March 1968, King reiterated the point that Dives, the rich man, "didn't go to hell because he was rich; Dives didn't realize that his wealth was his opportunity. It was his opportunity to bridge the gulf that separated him from his brother Lazarus," who was poor and sick and needy ("Remaining Awake," 216). The point seems to be that one can acquire wealth and property, so long as one is charitably oriented in the disposal of it. It is perhaps worth mentioning that this ethical stance does not appear to square with King's own ethical practices. Touched early on by Gandhi's vow of poverty, King was famously averse to acquiring any sort of property, much to the chagrin of his home life (see Garrow, *Bearing the Cross*, 114–115). In 1960, when he had to confront trumped-up charges of tax evasion in Montgomery, King proclaimed that, "I own just one piece of property, a 1954 Pontiac" (cited in Garrow, 129). Despite the occasional bourgeois preaching, we might say, the bourgeois label never really fit the man.

57. Quoted in Jackson, *From Civil Rights to Human Rights*, 304. See also King, "Three Evils of Society."

58. King, "Retail, Wholesale," 59.

59. King, "Speech at SCLC Staff Retreat" [1966], 14.

60. Dawson, *Black Visions*, 17–18, 273–280.

61. King, "Other America" [1968], 160–161.

62. See Marx and Engels, *Communist Manifesto*, 221.

63. King, "Speech at SCLC Staff Retreat" [1966], 20.

64. King, "Annual Report of the President," 11. See also King, *Where Do We Go from Here?*, 171–172.

65. King, "Speech at SCLC Staff Retreat" [1966], 23.

66. See, for example, King's remarks to the SCLC staff in 1968, which reflect his final position on jobs programs and guaranteed income: "We must demand, for instance, an emergency program to provide employment for everyone in need of a job, or, if a work program is impractical, a guaranteed annual income at levels that sustain life in decent circumstances" ("A New Sense of Direction").

67. King, "Speech at SCLC Staff Retreat" [1966], 23. See also King, *Where Do We Go from Here?*, 209. It is perhaps worth noting that King's redefinition of work and call for a guaranteed basic income shares similarities with, but also moves beyond, James Livingston's arguments against jobs programs. See Livingston, *No More Work*.

68. See, for example, King, "To Minister to the Valley."

69. For a cogent discussion of the U.S. Government's mortgage interest deduction as an example of this "socialism for the rich," see Desmond, "How Home Ownership Became the Engine of American Inequality." See also Cedric Durand's commentary on how, throughout the rich countries, state efforts to manage the 2008 financial crisis "led to the socialization of the costs of the financial collapse—indeed, on a scale never previously imagined—without the working classes or the unemployed ever feeling the supposed benefits of this 'communism for capital.'" Durand notes that "between autumn 2008 and the beginning of 2009, the total amount that states and central banks in the advanced countries committed to supporting the financial sector (through recapitalization, nationalization, repurchasing assets, loans, guarantees, injections of liquidity) has been evaluated at some 50.4 percent of world GDP!" (*Fictitious Capital*, 39).

70. See King's reflections on state support of white land acquisition in "The Other America" [1968], 165.

71. Myerson and Smith, "We'll Need an Economic Program to Make #BlackLivesMatter." Matthew Desmond's book-length study, *Evicted*, provides a vivid contemporary portrayal of precisely the sort of rent-based expropriation that so dearly troubled King more than a half-century ago.

72. On the Indian Bhoodan or Land Gift Movement of the 1950s, see King, "My Trip to the Land of Gandhi," 107. For a rich discussion of how Indian political and intellectual history factors into King's thinking and midcentury Black internationalism, see Immerwahr, "Caste or Colony?"

73. King, "Beyond Vietnam" 206–207.

74. *New York Times* Editorial Board, "Dr. King's Error," 36.

75. King, "Other America" [1968], 165.

76. King, "Beyond Vietnam" 213–214 (emphasis added).

77. Forged initially by the early-century contributions of Rosa Luxemburg, the critical theorization of military stimulus spending experienced a watershed moment in the late 1960s, with the publication of Baran and Sweezy's *Monopoly Capital*. See also Luxemburg, *Accumulation of Capital*.

78. Marx, *Capital*, 1:172, emphasis added.

79. Singh, *Race and America's Long War*, 79. See also Beckert, *Empire of Cotton*; Johnson, *River of Dark Dreams*; Baptist, *Half Has Never Been Told*; Blackburn, *Making of New World Slavery*.

80. Singh, *Race and America's Long War*, 79.

81. Singh, *Race and America's Long War*, 96–97.

82. Singh, *Race and America's Long War*, 96–97.

83. Amin, *Law of Worldwide Value*, 84.

84. Terry, "Requiem for a Dream." See also Rasberry, *Race and the Totalitarian Century*.

85. Terry, "Requiem for a Dream," 313.

86. Terry, "Requiem for a Dream," 315.

87. King, "'A Realistic Look,'" 175–176, emphasis added. King's commentary on the Bandung Conference and its aftermath can be read to parallel much of what Samir Amin has argued about Bandung and the global "Southern awakening" from roughly 1955 to the onset of the neoliberal period. See *Law of Worldwide Value*, 113–136.

88. King, "Beyond Vietnam," 215.

89. King, "New Sense of Direction." Here it is perhaps worth quoting the fuller passage: "It is difficult to exaggerate the creative contribution of dynamic young Negroes of the past eight years. They took non-violent resistance, first employed in Montgomery, Alabama, in mass dimensions and developed original applications—sit-ins, freedom rides and wade-ins. To accomplish these ends they first transformed themselves. Young Negroes had traditionally imitated whites in dress, conduct and thought in a rigid middle-class pattern. . . . Now they ceased imitating and began initiating. Leadership passed into the hands of Negroes, and their white allies began learning from them. This was a revolutionary and wholesome development for both. It is ironic that today so many educators and sociologists are seeking new methods to instill middle-class values in Negro youth as the ideal in social development. It was precisely when young Negroes threw off their middle-class values that they made an historic social contribution. They abandoned those values when they put careers and wealth in a secondary role, when they cheerfully became jailbirds and troublemakers. When they took off their Brooks Brothers attire and put on overalls to work in the isolated rural South, they challenged and inspired white youth to emulate them. Many left school, not to abandon learning but to seek it in more direct ways. They were constructive school dropouts, strengthening society and themselves. These Negro and white youths preceded the conception of the Peace Corps, and I think it is safe to say that their work inspired its organization on an international scale."

90. Holt, *Children of Fire*, 354, 357.

91. Clover, *Riot. Strike. Riot*, 29–30.

92. Clover, *Riot. Strike. Riot*, 21.

93. King, "Testament of Hope," 317.

94. See King, "National Labor Leadership Assembly for Peace," 143, and King, *Trumpet of Conscience*, 57–59: "The bloodlust interpretation [of the summer of 1967] ignores one of the most striking features of the city riots. Violent they certainly were. But the violence, to a startling degree, was focused against property rather than against people. There were very few cases of injury to persons, and the vast majority of the rioters were not involved in attacking people. The much-publicized 'death toll' that marked the riots, and the many injuries, were overwhelmingly inflicted on the rioters by the military. It is clear that the riots were exacerbated by police action that was designed to injure or even to kill people. . . . I am aware that there are many who wince at a distinction between property and persons—who hold both sacrosanct. My views are not so rigid. A life is sacred. Property is intended to serve life, and no matter how much we surround it with rights and respect, it has no personal being. . . . The focus on property in the 1967 riots is not accidental. It has a message; it is saying something. . . . Those people wanted the

experience of taking, of redressing the power imbalance that property represents. Possession, afterward, was secondary." We should note, too, that two points here compare favorably with Robinson's articulation of the nature of the Black radical tradition, namely, 1) the absence of mass violence and 2) the rejection, or revaluation, of Western ideas about property ownership (*Black Marxism*, 168). The question of violence and King's situation within the Black radical tradition is taken up in chapter four.

95. King, "Testament of Hope," 317.

96. See, for example, Levinson, *Extraordinary Time*; R. Gordon, *Rise and Fall of American Growth*; and Galbraith, *End of Normal*. Cf. Brenner, *Economics of Global Turbulence*; Streeck, *How Will Capitalism End?*; M. Roberts, *Long Depression*.

97. See Livingston, "Against Apocalypse Economics."

98. Jackson, From Civil Rights to Human Rights, 251.

Chapter Four. "Showdown for Nonviolence"

1. See, for example, the policy platform of the contemporary Movement for Black Lives: https://policy.m4bl.org/platform/.

2. Robinson, *Terms of Order*, 1.

3. Robinson, *Black Marxism*, 168; A. Gordon, preface to *An Anthropology of Marxism*," xi.

4. King, "Showdown for Nonviolence," 64.

5. King, "Speech to Mass Meeting," 171.

6. King, "Showdown for Nonviolence," 64–65. See also the National Advisory Commission on Civil Disorders, *Kerner Report*.

7. See Tillmon, "Welfare is a Women's Issue." "I'm a woman. I'm a black woman. I'm a poor woman. I'm a fat woman. I'm a middle-aged woman. And I'm on welfare. In this country, if you're any one of those things you count less as a human being. If you're all those things, you don't count at all. Except as a statistic.... There are millions of statistics like me." Tillmon goes on to say, in an oft-cited passage: "Welfare is like a super-sexist marriage. You trade in a man for the man. But you can't divorce him if he treats you bad. He can divorce you, of course, cut you off anytime he wants. But in that case, he keeps the kids, not you. The man runs everything.... You give up control of your own body... .. The man, the welfare system, controls your money. He tells you what to buy, what not to buy, where to buy it, and how much things cost. If things—rent, for instance—really cost more than he says they do, it's just too bad for you. He's always right."

8. Tillmon and King, quoted in Nadasen, *Welfare Warriors*, 72.

9. Laurent, *King and the Other America*, 170.

10. Laurent, *King and the Other America*, 170, 173. See also Nadasen, "'We Do Whatever Becomes Necessary,'" 326-327.

11. See Terry and Threadcraft, "Gender Trouble," and deGregory and Baldwin, "Sexism in the World House."

12. King, "Showdown for Nonviolence," 67, 68.

13. Fraser and Jaeggi, *Capitalism*, 31.

14. Fraser and Jaeggi, *Capitalism*, 89.

15. Fraser and Jaeggi, *Capitalism*, 85.

16. King, "Greatest Hope for World Peace," 149.

17. Myrdal, *International Economy*.

18. See Getachew, *Worldmaking after Empire*. Getachew documents how in the ideas behind the New International Economic Order (NIEO) of the 1970s, in particular the intellectual and political leadership of Julius Nyerere in Tanzania and Michael Manley in Jamaica, reflected an extension of Myrdal's "welfare world" thesis.

19. Myrdal, *An International Economy*, 324.

20. Moyn, "Welfare World," 175–176.

21. See the discussions of how the AFL-CIO—including its Black worker organizing apparatus, the A. Philip Randolph Institute—remained staunchly opposed to King's critique of U.S. foreign policy in Laurent, *King and the Other America*, 144–145, and Honey, *To the Promised Land*, 104–105.

22. Getachew, *Worldmaking after Empire*, 163.

23. "What does it profit a man to be able to eat at an integrated lunch counter if he doesn't earn enough money to buy a hamburger and a cup of coffee?" (King, "All Labor Has Dignity," 175).

24. Getachew, *Worldmaking after Empire*, 166–167.

25. Moyn, "Welfare World," 180.

26. See, for example, King, "Birth of a New Nation," 58–75.

27. For a more comprehensive account of King's theory of the state, what we refer to as his conventional conception of the political, see Long, *Against Us, But for Us*.

28. Robinson, *Terms of Order*, 20.

29. Cited in Garrow, *Bearing the Cross*, 488.

30. King, *Where Do We Go from Here?*, 144.

31. Cited in Garrow, *Bearing the Cross*, 488.

32. Quan, "'It's Hard to Stop Rebels That Time Travel,'" 174.

33. Fluker, "They Looked for a City," 39.

34. Jensen and King, "Beloved Community," 16.

35. Quan, "'It's Hard to Stop Rebels That Time Travel,'" 175.

36. King, "Showdown for Nonviolence," 69.

37. Robinson, *Terms of Order*, 214–215.

38. Harding, *Martin Luther King*, 48–49. On the point about socialisms "that we have seen," clearly King's rejection of communism was motivated by a concern about the state-centered conception of the political. But, to be sure, King is far more ambiguous and ambivalent in regard to democratic socialism. Michael Long has argued, in contrast to Harding, that King's praise of the Scandinavian welfare states in the mid-1960s is evidence of his affirmation of the "good state," or his affirmation that the state-centered conception of the political could be redeemed as a "trustee of the beloved community."

Long, who has written the only book-length study of King's theory of the state, contends that while King was well attuned to the lived realities of state repression, he did not believe that coercive violence was the defining nature of the modern state as such. "As part of a family subjected to political repression, as one who was repeatedly jailed for disobeying unjust laws, and as a leader of those who suffered state-sanctioned brutalities, King was well aware of the tendency of the state to transform itself into a repressive police state, and so chose carefully not to provide any ontological grounding that might sanction an understanding of the state as primarily a coercive power. Thus King grounded the state in human sociality, a move that easily enabled him to call upon the state to be more than a jailer" (*Against Us, But For Us*, 219). Our driving point in this chapter is just that King's political imaginary exceeded the presumption of state governability.

39. Harding, *Martin Luther King*, 48–49, emphasis added.

40. Harding, *Martin Luther King*, 100–101. Harding refers to a "certain logic" in "the vision of a man who had committed himself unequivocally to the empowerment of the poor, to the transformation of the nation, away from racism, from militarism and materialism, toward a more humane and compassionate *way of life*" (100, emphasis added). Harding, who coauthored King's legendary 1967 antiwar speech and developed a profound connection with King in the final years, is remembering and celebrating not any appeal to new ways of being governed, but rather an appeal to a new way of life.

41. One is reminded here of Robinson's introduction to his chapter on the "nature" of the Black radical tradition: "This brings us finally to the character, or more accurately to the ideological, philosophical, and epistemological natures of the Black movement whose dialectical matrix we believe was capitalist slavery and imperialism" (*Black Marxism*, 167).

42. Robinson, *Black Marxism*, 168.

43. Robinson, *Black Marxism*, 168.

44. King, "Showdown for Nonviolence," 70.

45. Robinson, *Black Marxism*, 168–169.

46. For a discussion of Du Bois's conservationist argument and its parallels with King's later thinking, see Douglas, *W. E. B. Du Bois and the Critique of the Competitive Society*.

47. Robinson, *Terms of Order*, 150. See also Erica Edwards on the tensions inherent in Black charismatic leadership, which captures something of the layered nature of King's two conceptions of the political: "One of the founding problematics of a black political modernity in the making is this double potential of the charismatic leadership role: to discipline, on the one hand, and to disrupt, precisely by way of charismatic performance, the disciplinary machinations of the capitalist order on the other" (*Charisma and the Fictions of Black Leadership*, 5). Also relevant here is Carson, "Martin Luther King, Jr."

48. Robinson, *Black Movements in America*, 144.

49. For a recent account of how King's patriarchal notions of movement leadership compare with theories of movement leadership today, see Kauffman, *How to Read a Protest*.

50. Baker, *Betrayal*.

51. See Dellinger, "Last March of Martin Luther King."

52. Nadasen, *Welfare Warriors*, 72.

53. King, "All Labor Has Dignity," 177. See also Honey, *To the Promised Land*, 157. For a discussion, in the context of the Black radical tradition, of "the general strike as refusing to bargain and plead with the state and instead simply refusing it outright," see Martel, "Stages of Freedom."

54. Quan, "'It's Hard to Stop Rebels That Time Travel,'" 174, emphasis added.

55. Robinson, *Black Marxism*, xxx, emphasis added.

56. Robinson, "Notes toward a 'Native' Theory of History," 47.

57. Edwards, foreword, *Terms of Order*, xviii.

58. See Long, *Against Us, But for Us*, 73.

59. Dorrien, *Breaking White Supremacy*, 3.

60. Dorrien, *Breaking White Supremacy*, 18.

61. King, "Honoring Dr. Du Bois," 113.

62. King, "Honoring Dr. Du Bois," 117.

63. Robinson, *Black Marxism*, 169; Robinson, *Terms of Order*, 1.

64. See Jensen and King, "Beloved Community." See also Greg Burris's reference to the "quasi-mystical dimension of Robinson's work," which "is most apparent in those moments when he dips into theology" ("Birth of a [Zionist] Nation," 131).

65. Lipsitz, "What Is This Black in the Black Radical Tradition?," 108.

66. King, "Showdown for Nonviolence," 69. King's fears were warranted. Consider the case of the Attica Prison uprising of 1971. Heather Ann Thompson has shown how the Attica insurrection at the hands of Black inmates, which gripped the nation's attention for four days and resulted in 43 deaths, had a marked impact on white consciousness and contributed significantly to the emergence of more repressive criminal justice policies and practices, ultimately what has come to be known as the New Jim Crow, which has had devastating consequences on Black communities in the United States (see *Blood in the Water*).

67. Here it is worth emphasizing that King seems to have thought that moral sensitivity to suffering was affected by historical development in material capacity. In *Where Do We Go from Here?*, for example, he argued that "what followed the Civil War was morally *worse* than the crimes that precipitated it" (248). We take this to mean, at least in part, that the expansion of state access and provision during Reconstruction thereby expanded the moral field, rendering the continued denial of rights and resources both morally problematic and morally urgent in ways that it had not been, could not have been, prior to that historical precedent.

68. Mantena, "Showdown for Nonviolence," 80.

69. Mantena, "Showdown for Nonviolence," 92.

70. On King's vision for the persistence of racial identity in a radically transformed society, that is, his rejection of a "colorblind" vision of the beloved community, see Sundstrom, "Prophetic Tension."

71. See Robinson, *Black Marxism*, 169. See also Robinson's later essay, "In Search of a Pan-African Commonwealth," 161–169. In trying to imagine a Pan-Africanism that could confront the neoliberal entrenchment of the transnational capitalist elite and "rupture the boundaries drawn by national sovereignty and imperial ambitions," Robinson suggests that "the Pan-Africanist movement must now collude with these opportune supra-national pressures." Drawing on the cultural and revolutionary Pan-Africanism "employed and articulated by James, Padmore, Nkrumah, Nyerere, Cabral, Fanon, and more frequently and significantly the anonymous black masses which confronted slavery, colonialism and imperialism on the ground in Africa and the Diaspora," any potential "Pan-African Commonwealth must seek to fulfil Sekou Toure's (1974) recognition that 'Since revolutionary Pan-Africanism basically refers to an Africa of Peoples, it is in its interest to uphold the primacy of peoples as against States.'" One wonders how King's appeal to a "new kind of togetherness" might be said to bear on his own Pan-African vision, and whether or not we might situate King in this pantheon.

72. King, "Statement on the Poor People's Campaign."

73. It is worth pointing out that while the neoliberal empowerment of private capital might appear to align with a call for "ungovernability," it is, as Quan puts it, a form of "ungovernability from above," one that must be distinguished from democratic struggles for "ungovernability from below" and one that "cannot be equated with the absence of governing." Quan goes on to point out that "neoliberal state actors typically seek to dismantle whatever remnants are left of the social welfare contract so that ruling apparatuses appear to take on . . . the antistate state form. . . . The antistate antics displayed by many state actors are political theater and should not be confused with the absence of governing from the top" ("'It's Hard to Stop Rebels That Time Travel,'" 179n29).

74. Fraser and Jaeggi, *Capitalism*, 76, 80–81.

75. Dawson, "Future of Black Politics."

76. Dorrien, *Breaking White Supremacy*, 426.

77. Fraser, "Behind Marx's Hidden Abode," 58.

Chapter Five. "Liberated Grounds on Which to Gather"

1. Terry, "Requiem for a Dream."

2. White, *Challenge of Blackness*.

3. Harding, "Vocation," 14.

4. White, "Institute of the Black World."

5. See R. Ferguson, *Reorder of Things*, 18.

6. Harney and Moten, *Undercommons*, 26. See also Kelley, "Black Study, Black Struggle."

7. Harding, "Vocation," 11.

8. Rodney, *Groundings with My Brothers*, 67; Harding, "Vocation," 6. On Rodney's work with the IBW, see Rodney, *Walter Rodney Speaks*.

9. Harding, "Vocation," 13, 6.

10. Harding, "Vocation," 6.

11. Payne, *I've Got the Light of Freedom*, 93. On Baker's criticism of King, see Ransby, *Ella Baker*, 189–192.

12. Ransby, *Ella Baker*, 5.

13. Ransby, *Ella Baker*, 92.

14. See Gooding-Williams, *In the Shadow of Du Bois*, 166–168.

15. Ransby, *Ella Baker*, 327.

16. Horton and Freire, *We Make the Road by Walking*, 44.

17. Levine, "Birth of the Citizenship Schools," 414.

18. See Horton, "Roots of Southern Radicalism," 10.

19. King, "'Look to the Future,'" 7.

20. For recent commentaries on this well-documented history, see Laurent, *King and the Other America*, 153–154, and Honey, *To the Promised Land*, 49–52.

21. Cited in White, "Audacious Visions," 4.

22. King, "Honoring Dr. Du Bois," 113.

23. Harding, "Vocation," 8.

24. Harding, "Vocation," 20.

25. See Robinson's articulation of the "nature of the Black radical tradition" (Robinson, *Black Marxism*, 168–169). Harding cites Frantz Fanon, who in a personal letter to a friend written just days before he died, said that "we are nothing on earth if we are not first of all slaves to a cause" ("Vocation," 28). On this connection between the IBW and Robinson's formulation of the Black radical tradition, see White, *Challenge of Blackness*, 200–202.

26. Robinson, *Black Marxism*, 316.

27. Harding, "Vocation," 26.

28. This is not to suggest that Harding's initial efforts with the King Center, where he was tapped to initiate the Library Documentation Project, were ever flush with cash. "We originally had big dreams that all the guilty white folks all over the country would be contributing pounds of money to the Martin Luther King Center," Harding said in 1970. "That was not the case, because they didn't feel as guilty as I thought" (See Poinsett, "Think Tank for Black Scholars," 47). See also Derrick White's account of Harding's work with the King Center and its fundraising challenges (*Challenge of Blackness*, 74–86).

29. See Allen, *Black Awakening in Capitalist America*, 75–77. Allen cites Ford Foundation president Henry Heald, who in 1965 communicated in no uncertain terms his desire to use public-private partnerships to push an investment-oriented agenda. Note that JCPS later became the Joint Center for Political and Economic Studies and is frequently referred to simply as the "Joint Center."

30. Allen, *Black Awakening in Capitalist America*, 76.

31. It is worth quoting at length Derrick White's very helpful summarization of the tensions between the King Center and the IBW: "The IBW's separation from the

King Center occurred because the latter insisted on a narrow racial liberalism from all of its components, reflecting its larger goal of becoming the official interpreter of King's life and legacy. The King Center provided the IBW with physical space, but over the course of 1970, its board of directors also demanded strict ideological adherence to civil rights liberalism. The IBW and the King Center's differences reflect larger issues regarding the interpretation of King's life and legacy. After his assassination, a variety of groups sought to explain the significance of King's life and activism. The mainstream press emphasized his 'dream' and nonviolent action against the backdrop of urban rebellions and Black Power militancy. The SCLC stressed King's aggressive nonviolent activism, which they continued in a variety of campaigns after his death. Harding approached King's life from a nuanced perspective, one that accepted his religious ecumenicism and his radicalism in terms of peace, poverty, and racial pride. These somewhat conflicting interpretations formed the basis of a contested historical memory. The King Center, under Coretta Scott King's leadership, sought to be the official voice and interpreter of King. In this process, the center and its commitment to commemoration were essential. The center echoed the mainstream media's interpretation by focusing on King's belief in nonviolence and by making the March on Washington the centerpiece of the historical narrative. This decision, rooted in ideology and memory, reduced or eliminated King's ideas on poverty, militarism, and racial pride. King's views expressed in *Where Do We Go from Here: Chaos of Community?*—such as a guaranteed income, universal healthcare, and the importance of racial pride—were, perhaps deliberately, marginalized for the sake of a broadly approved and supported memorial. The center's board required a narrow, King-centered historical interpretation of the civil rights movement. Any King Center component that deviated from this narrative faced intense scrutiny and, ultimately, contraction" (*Challenge of Blackness*, 60–61).

32. Harding, "Vocation," 15, 13.

33. Harding, "Vocation," 15.

34. Clark, Myrdal, and Wilson, *Dark Ghetto*, 11.

35. Harris-Hurd, "Keeping Tabs," 31.

36. Harris-Hurd, "Keeping Tabs," 32–33.

37. Harding and Strickland, "For a Black Political Agenda," 27.

38. See Harding, cited in White, *Challenge of Blackness*, 125; Institute of the Black World, "Report of Political Organizing Task Force," cited in White, *Challenge of Blackness*, 112.

39. See Rodriguez, "Political Logic," 21–22.

40. Rodriguez, "Political Logic," 23.

41. See White, *Challenge of Blackness*, 84.

42. For an account of the IBW's pedagogical work and involvement in the Attica prison uprisings of 1971, see Grady-Willis, *Challenging U.S. Apartheid*, 164.

43. White, *Challenge of Blackness*, 19–50.

44. Harding, "Toward the Black University," 157.

45. Harding, "Toward the Black University," 157. See also the discussion of Harding's vision and its precursors in Douglas, *W. E. B. Du Bois*, 65–90.

46. Harding, "Toward the Black University," 158.

47. See Benson, *Fighting for Our Place*, and Rickford, *We Are an African People*.

48. For helpful commentaries on student demands for Black studies programming and the reactionary postures of historically Black college and university (HBCU) administrators and trustees, in the 1960s and well into the era of neoliberalism, see R. Ferguson, *We Demand,* and Myers, *We Are Worth Fighting For.*

49. White, *Challenge of Blackness*, 41.

50. Harding, "Toward the Black University," 159.

51. Harding, "Vocation," 6.

52. Wilder, *Ebony and Ivy*.

53. Boggs and Mitchell, "Critical University Studies," 452.

54. Boggs and Mitchell, "Critical University Studies," 452–453.

55. paperson, *Third University*, 32.

56. "The walls of the academy," Harding said in "Vocation," are, "on the whole, merely more tastefully, delicately wrought extensions of the walls of the government, industry, and the military" (4).

57. paperson, *Third University*, xiv.

58. paperson, *Third University*, xiv–xv, 36.

59. paperson, *Third University*, 42.

60. paperson, *Third University*, xvii, xxiii.

61. paperson, *Third University*, 36.

62. Harney and Moten, *Undercommons*, 26.

63. Harney and Moten refer to the sociality of the undercommons as a form of "prophetic organization" (*Undercommons*, 27, 31), which bears a striking resemblance to appeals to prophetic sociality in the late 1960s. See, for example, Gerald McWorter, who emphasized "*the prophetic social role of the Black University*" ("Nature and Needs of the Black University," 6).

64. Harding, "Vocation," 24.

65. Boggs "Think Dialectically," 266.

66. Harney and Moten, *Undercommons*, 110–111.

67. Harney and Moten, *Undercommons*, 111.

68. Harding, "Prof. Vincent Harding on Martin Luther King," 93.

69. paperson, *Third University*, 32.

70. Kelley, "Black Study, Black Struggle."

71. Harney and Moten, *Undercommons*, 133. For a generative discussion of how Sylvia Wynter came to reflect on this very problematic during her time at the IBW, and in the process reckoned with Marxism and the Black radical tradition, see White, "Black Metamorphosis."

72. Brown, *Edgework*, 11.

73. King, *Where Do We Go from Here?*, 179.

74. King, "If the Negro Wins, Labor Wins," 37.
75. See Jackson, *From Civil Rights to Human Rights*, 331.
76. King, "Testament of Hope," 315.
77. See, for example, King, "To the Mountaintop," 192–195.
78. King, "Speech at SCLC Staff Retreat" [1967].
79. King, "Speech at SCLC Staff Retreat" [1967].

BIBLIOGRAPHY

Akuno, Kali, and Ajamu Nangwaya. *Jackson Rising: The Struggle for Economic Democracy and Black Self-Determination in Jackson, Mississippi*. Montreal: Daraja Press, 2017.

Allen, Robert L. *Black Awakening in Capitalist America: An Analytic History*. 1969. Trenton, NJ: Africa World Press, 1990.

Amin, Samir. *The Law of Worldwide Value*. New York: Monthly Review, 2010.

Ansbro, John J. *Martin Luther King, Jr.: The Making of a Mind*. Lanham, MD: Madison Books, 2000.

Baker, Houston A., Jr. *Betrayal: How Black Intellectuals Have Abandoned the Ideals of the Civil Rights Era*. New York: Columbia University Press, 2008.

Baldwin, Lewis V. *There Is a Balm in Gilead: The Cultural Roots of Martin Luther King, Jr.* Minneapolis: Fortress Press, 1991.

———. *The Voice of Conscience: The Church in the Mind of Martin Luther King, Jr.* New York: Oxford University Press, 2010.

Baptist, Edward E. *The Half Has Never Been Told: Slavery and the Making of American Capitalism*. New York: Basic, 2016.

Baran, Paul A., and Paul Sweezy. *Monopoly Capital: An Essay on the American Economic and Social Order*. New York: Monthly Review, 1966.

Beckert, Sven. *Empire of Cotton: A Global History*. New York: Vintage, 2015.

Belafonte, Harry, and Michael Shnayerson. *My Song: A Memoir of Art, Race, and Defiance*. New York: Random House, 2012.

Benson, Richard, II. *Fighting for Our Place in the Sun: Malcolm X and the Radicalization of the Black Student Movement 1960–1973*. New York: Peter Lang, 2014.

Berdyaev, N. A. "Marx and Personalism." *Christendom*, no. 2 (December 1935).

Blackburn, Robin. *The Making of New World Slavery: From the Baroque to the Modern: 1492–1800*. New York: Verso, 2010.

Bloom, Joshua, and Waldo E. Martin. *Black against Empire: The History and Politics of the Black Panther Party*. Oakland: University of California Press, 2016.

Boggs, Abigail, and Nick Mitchell. "Critical University Studies and the Crisis Consensus." *Feminist Studies* 44, no. 2 (2018): 432–463.

Boggs, James. "Think Dialectically, Not Biologically." In *Pages from a Black Radical's Notebook: A James Boggs Reader*, edited by Stephen M. Ward, 264–273. Detroit: Wayne State University Press, 2011.

Branch, Taylor. *Parting the Waters: America in the King Years 1954–63.* New York: Simon and Shuster, 1989.

Brenner, Robert. *The Economics of Global Turbulence: The Advanced Capitalist Economies from Long Boom to Long Downturn, 1945–2005.* New York: Verso, 2006.

Brown, Wendy. *Edgework: Critical Essays on Knowledge and Politics.* Princeton, NJ: Princeton University Press, 2009.

Burris, Greg. "Birth of a (Zionist) Nation: Black Radicalism and the Future of Palestine." In *Futures of Black Radicalism*, edited by Gaye Theresa Johnson and Alex Lubin, 120–132. New York: Verso, 2018.

Burrow, Rufus, Jr. *God and Human Dignity: The Personalism, Theology, and Ethics of Martin Luther King, Jr.* South Bend, IN: University of Notre Dame Press, 2006.

Carson, Clayborne. "Martin Luther King, Jr.: Charismatic Leadership in a Mass Struggle." *Journal of American History* 74, no. 2 (September 1987): 448–454.

Chakravartty, Paula, and Denise Ferreira da Silva. "Accumulation, Dispossession, and Debt: The Racial Logic of Global Capitalism—an Introduction." *American Quarterly* 64, no. 3 (2012): 361–385.

Chen, Chris. "The Limit Point of Capitalist Equality." *Endnotes 3: Gender, Race, Class and Other Misfortunes* (September 2013).

Ciccariello-Maher, George. *Decolonizing Dialectics.* Durham, NC: Duke University Press, 2016.

Clark, Kenneth B., Gunnar Myrdal, and William Julius Wilson. *Dark Ghetto: Dilemmas of Social Power.* 1965. Middletown, CT: Wesleyan University Press, 1989.

Clarno, Andy. *Neoliberal Apartheid: Palestine/Israel and South Africa after 1994.* Chicago: University of Chicago Press, 2017.

Clover, Joshua. *Riot. Strike. Riot: The New Era of Uprisings.* New York: Verso, 2016.

Cox, Oliver C. *Capitalism as a System.* New York: Monthly Review, 1964.

Cunningham, Nijah. "A Queer Pier: Roundtable on the Idea of a Black Radical Tradition." *Small Axe* 17, no. 1 (2013): 84–95.

Dawson, Michael C. *Blacks In and Out of the Left.* Cambridge, MA: Harvard University Press, 2013.

———. *Black Visions: The Roots of Contemporary African-American Political Ideologies.* Chicago: University of Chicago Press, 2001.

———. "The Future of Black Politics." *Boston Review* 37, 1 (January–February 2012). http://bostonreview.net/archives/BR37.1/ndf_michael_dawson_black_politics.php.

———. "Hidden in Plain Sight: A Note on Legitimation Crises and the Racial Order." *Critical Historical Studies* 3, no. 1 (Spring 2016): 143–161.

Degregory, Crystal A., and Lewis V. Baldwin. "Sexism in the World House: Women and the Global Vision of Martin Luther King Jr." In *Reclaiming the Great World House: The Global Vision of Martin Luther King Jr.*, edited by Vicki L. Crawford and Lewis V. Baldwin, 107–132. Athens: University of Georgia Press, 2019.

Dellinger, Drew. "The Last March of Martin Luther King." *The Atlantic*, April 4, 2018. https://www.theatlantic.com/politics/archive/2018/04/mlk-last-march/555953/.

Denning, Michael. "Wageless Life." *New Left Review* 66 (November–December 2010): 79–97.

Desmond, Matthew. *Evicted: Poverty and Profit in the American City*. New York: Crown, 2016.

———. "How Home Ownership Became the Engine of American Inequality." *New York Times Magazine*, May 9, 2017. https://www.nytimes.com/2017/05/09 /magazine/how-homeownership-became-the-engine-of-american-inequality .html?_r=0.

Dorrien, Gary. *Breaking White Supremacy: Martin Luther King Jr. and the Black Social Gospel*. New Haven, CT: Yale University Press, 2018.

Douglas, Andrew J. "'The Brutal Dialectics of Underdevelopment': Thinking Politically with Walter Rodney." *C.L.R. James Journal* 23, nos. 1–2 (2017): 245–266.

———. *In the Spirit of Critique: Thinking Politically in the Dialectical Tradition*. Albany: State University of New York Press, 2013.

———. *W. E. B. Du Bois and the Critique of the Competitive Society*. Athens: University of Georgia Press, 2019.

Dreier, Peter. "Martin Luther King Was A Democratic Socialist." *The Huffington Post*, January 18, 2016. http://www.huffingtonpost.com/peter-dreier/martin -luther-king-was-a-democratic-socialist_b_9008990.html.

Drezner, Daniel. *The Ideas Industry: How Pessimists, Partisans, and Plutocrats are transforming the Marketplace of Ideas*. New York: Oxford University Press, 2017.

Du Bois, W. E. B. *Black Reconstruction in America, 1860–1880*. 1935. New York: Free Press, 1997.

———. *The Souls of Black Folk*. 1903. New York: Oxford University Press, 2007.

Durand, Cedric. *Fictitious Capital: How Finance Is Appropriating Our Future*. New York: Verso, 2017.

Edwards, Erica R. *Charisma and the Fictions of Black Leadership*. Minneapolis: University of Minnesota Press, 2012.

———. Foreword to *The Terms of Order: Political Science and the Myth of Leadership*, by Cedric J. Robinson, ix–xxvii. Chapel Hill: University of North Carolina Press, 2016.

Endnotes Collective. "Misery and Debt." *Endnotes 2: Misery and the Value Form* (April 2010).

Ezra, Michael, ed. *The Economic Civil Rights Movement: African Americans and the Struggle for Economic Power*. New York: Routledge, 2013.

Fairclough, Adam. "Was Martin Luther King a Marxist?" *History Workshop* 15 (Spring 1983): 117–125.

Fanon, Frantz. *Black Skin, White Masks*. 1952. Translated by Richard Philcox. New York: Grove Press, 2008.

———. *The Wretched of the Earth*. 1961. Translated by Richard Philcox. New York: Grove Press, 2005.

Ferguson, Stephen C., II. "The Philosopher King: An Examination of the Influence of Dialectics on King's Political Thought and Practice." In *The Liberatory Thought of*

Martin Luther King, Jr.: Critical Essays on the Philosopher King, edited by Robert E. Birt, 87–108. Lanham, MD: Lexington Books, 2012.

Ferguson, Roderick. *The Reorder of Things: The University and Its Pedagogies of Minority Difference.* Minneapolis: University of Minnesota Press, 2012.

———. *We Demand: The University and Student Protests.* Oakland: University of California Press, 2017.

Finley, Mary Lou, Bernard LaFayette Jr., James R. Ralph Jr., and Pam Smith, eds. *The Chicago Freedom Movement: Martin Luther King Jr. and Civil Rights Activism in the North.* Lexington: University Press of Kentucky, 2016.

Fluker, Walter Earl. "They Looked for a City: A Comparison of the Ideal of Community in Howard Thurman and Martin Luther King, Jr." *Journal of Religious Ethics* 18, no. 2 (Spring 1990): 33–55.

Fraser, Nancy. "Behind Marx's Hidden Abode: For an Expanded Conception of Capitalism." *New Left Review* 86 (March–April 2014): 55–72.

———. "Expropriation and Exploitation in Racialized Capitalism: A Reply to Michael Dawson." *Critical Historical Studies* 3, no. 1 (Spring 2016): 163–178.

Fraser, Nancy, and Rahel Jaeggi. *Capitalism: A Conversation in Critical Theory.* Medford, MA: Polity Press, 2018.

Galbraith, James K. *The End of Normal: The Great Crisis and the Future of Growth.* New York: Simon and Schuster, 2015.

Garrow, David J. *Bearing the Cross: Martin Luther King, Jr., and the Southern Christian Leadership Conference.* New York: Harper Collins, 2004.

Getachew, Adom. *Worldmaking after Empire: The Rise and Fall of Self-Determination.* Princeton, NJ: Princeton University Press, 2019.

Geuss, Raymond. *Philosophy and Real Politics.* Princeton, NJ: Princeton University Press, 2008.

Gilmore, Glenda. *Defying Dixie: The Radical Roots of Civil Rights, 1919–1950.* New York: Norton, 2009.

Gilmore, Ruth Wilson. "Race and Globalization." In *Geographies of Global Change: Remapping the World*, edited by R. J. Johnson, Peter J. Taylor, and Michael J. Watts, 261–274. New York: Wiley-Blackwell, 2002.

Gooding-Williams, Robert. *In the Shadow of Du Bois: Afro-Modern Political Thought in America.* Cambridge, MA: Harvard University Press, 2011.

Gordon, Avery. Preface to *An Anthropology of Marxism*, by Cedric J. Robinson, vii–xxii. Burlington, VT: Ashgate, 2001.

Gordon, Robert J. *The Rise and Fall of American Growth: The U. S. Standard of Living since the Civil War.* Princeton, NJ: Princeton University Press, 2016.

Grady-Willis, A. *Challenging U.S. Apartheid: Atlanta and Black Struggles for Human Rights, 1960–1977.* Durham, NC: Duke University Press, 2006.

Hall, Jacquelyn Dowd. "The Long Civil Rights Movement and the Political Uses of the Past." *Journal of American History* 91, no. 4 (2005): 1233–1263.

Harding, Vincent. *Martin Luther King: An Inconvenient Hero.* Maryknoll, NY: Orbis, 2008.

————. "Prof. Vincent Harding on Martin Luther King." *Peace Research* 29, no. 1 (February 1997): 90–99.

————. "Toward the Black University." *Ebony* 25, no. 10 (Aug. 1970): 113–117.

————. "The Vocation of the Black Scholar and the Struggles of the Black Community." In *Education and Black Struggle: Notes from the Colonized World*, 3–20. Atlanta: Institute of the Black World, 1974.

Harding, Vincent, and William Strickland. "For a Black Political Agenda." *The New York Times*, December 23, 1970.

Harney, Stefano, and Fred Moten. *The Undercommons: Fugitive Planning & Black Study*. Minor Compositions, 2013.

Harrington, Michael. *The Other America: Poverty in the United States*. 1962. New York: Scribner, 1997.

Harris-Hurd, Laura. "Keeping Tabs on Black Politics." *Black Enterprise* 8, no. 6 (1978): 31–35.

Harvey, David. *A Companion to Marx's* Capital. New York: Verso, 2010.

————. *The Limits to Capital*. New York: Verso, 2006.

————. *The New Imperialism*. New York: Oxford University Press, 2003.

————. *Seventeen Contradictions and the End of Capitalism*. New York: Oxford University Press, 2014.

Heideman, Paul, and Jonah Birch. "The Trouble with Anti-Antiracism." *Jacobin*, October 11, 2016. https://www.jacobinmag.com/2016/10/adolph-reed-blm-racism -capitalism-labor/.

Holt, Thomas C. *Children of Fire: A History of African Americans*: New York: Hill and Wang, 2010.

Honey, Michael K., ed. *"All Labor Has Dignity."* Boston: Beacon, 2011.

————. *Going Down Jericho Road: The Memphis Strike, Martin Luther King's Last Campaign*. New York: Norton, 2007.

————. Introduction to "To the Mountaintop" [1968] by Martin Luther King Jr. In *"All Labor Has Dignity,"* edited by Michael K. Honey. Boston: Beacon, 2011.

————. *To the Promised Land: Martin Luther King and the Fight for Economic Justice*: New York: Norton, 2018.

Horton, Myles. "The Roots of Southern Radicalism." In *The Myles Horton Reader: Education for Social Change*. Knoxville: University of Tennessee Press, 2003.

Horton, Myles, and Paulo Freire. *We Make the Road by Walking: Conversations on Education and Social Change*, edited by Brenda Bell, John Gaventa, and John Peters. Philadelphia: Temple University Press, 1990.

Immerwahr, Daniel. "Caste or Colony? Indianizing Race in the United States." *Modern Intellectual History* 4, no. 2 (2007): 275–301.

INCITE! Women of Color Against Violence. *The Revolution Will Not Be Funded: Beyond the Non-Profit Industrial Complex*. Durham, NC: Duke University Press, 2017.

Jackson, Thomas F. *From Civil Rights to Human Rights: Martin Luther King, Jr., and the Struggle for Economic Justice*. Philadelphia: University of Pennsylvania Press, 2009.

Jackson, Troy. *Becoming King: Martin Luther King, Jr., and the Making of a National Leader.* Lexington: University Press of Kentucky, 2008.

James, C. L. R. *Notes on Dialectics: Hegel, Marx, Lenin.* 1948. Westport, CT: Lawrence Hill, 1980.

———. "A Visit with Martin Luther King, March 25, 1957." https://solidarity-us.org /a-visit-with-martin-luther-king-jr/.

Jameson, Frederic. "Persistencies of the Dialectic: Three Sites." *Science and Society* 62, no. 3 (Fall 1998): 358–372.

———. *Valences of the Dialectic.* New York: Verso, 2009.

Jensen, Kipton, and Preston King. "Beloved Community: Martin Luther King, Howard Thurman, Josiah Royce." *Amity: The Journal of Friendship Studies* 4, no. 1 (2017): 16–31.

Johnson, Walter. *River of Dark Dreams: Slavery and Empire in the Cotton Kingdom.* Cambridge: Harvard University Press, 2017.

Kauffman, L.A. *How to Read a Protest: The Art of Organizing and Resistance.* Oakland: University of California Press, 2018.

Kelley, Robin D. G. "Black Study, Black Struggle." *Boston Review,* March 1, 2016. http://bostonreview.net/forum/robin-d-g-kelley-black-study-black-struggle.

———. "Coates and West in Jackson." *Boston Review,* December 22, 2017. http:// bostonreview.net/race/robin-d-g-kelley-coates-and-west-jackson (accessed June 25, 2019).

———. Introduction to *Race, Capitalism, Justice: Forum I,* edited by Walter Johnson and Robin D. G. Kelley, 5-8. Cambridge: Boston Review/MIT Press, 2017.

Khan-Cullors, Patrisse, and asha bandele, *When They Call You a Terrorist.* New York: St. Martin's Press, 2018.

King, Martin Luther, Jr. "All Labor Has Dignity" [1968]. In *"All Labor Has Dignity,"* edited by Michael K. Honey, 167-178. Boston: Beacon Press, 2011.

———. "Along this Way: The Violence of Poverty." *New York Amsterdam News,* January 1, 1966. http://thekingcenter.org/archive/document/along-way-violence-poverty.

———. "Annual Report of the President: Dr. Martin Luther King, Jr." [1967]. The Archives of the King Center for Nonviolent Social Change, Atlanta, Georgia.

———. *The Autobiography of Martin Luther King, Jr.,* edited by Clayborne Carson. New York: Warner Books, 2001.

———. "'Beyond Condemnation,' Sermon at Dexter Avenue Baptist Church" [1954]. In *The Papers of Martin Luther King, Jr., Volume VI: Advocate of the Social Gospel, September 1948–March 1963,* edited by Clayborne Carson, 199–201. Berkeley: University of California Press, 2007.

———. "Beyond Vietnam: A Time to Break Silence" [1967]. In *The Radical King,* edited by Cornel West, 201–220. Boston: Beacon, 2015.

———. "The Birth of a New Nation" [1957]. In *"A Single Garment of Destiny": A Global Vision of Justice,* edited by Lewis V. Baldwin, 58–75. Boston: Beacon, 2012.

———. "The Drum Major Instinct" [1968]. In *The Radical King,* edited by Cornel West, 253–264. Boston: Beacon, 2015.

————. "Freedom's Crisis: The Last Steep Ascent." *The Nation* 202, no. 11 (March 14, 1966): 288–292.

————. "The Greatest Hope for World Peace" [1964]. In *"A Single Garment of Destiny"": A Global Vision of Justice*, edited by Lewis V. Baldwin, 146–149. Boston: Beacon, 2012.

————. "Honoring Dr. Du Bois" [1968]. In *The Radical King*, edited by Cornel West, 113–121. Boston: Beacon, 2015.

————. "If the Negro Wins, Labor Wins" [1961]. In *"All Labor Has Dignity,"* edited by Michael K. Honey, 31–46. Boston: Beacon, 2011.

————. "'Let My People Go' South Africa Benefit Speech" [1965]. In *"In a Single Garment of Destiny": A Global Vision of Justice,* edited by Lewis V. Baldwin, 39–44. Boston: Beacon, 2012.

————. "Letter from Birmingham City Jail" [1963]. In *A Testament of Hope: The Essential Writings of Martin Luther King, Jr.,* edited by James. M. Washington, 289–302. New York: Harper and Row, 1986.

————. "'A Look to the Future,' Address Delivered at Highlander Folk School's Twenty-Fifth Anniversary Meeting" [1957]. In *"All Labor Has Dignity,"* edited by Michael K. Honey, 3–18. Boston: Beacon, 2011.

————. "The Man Who Was a Fool" [1961]. In *A Gift of Love: Sermons from* Strength to Love *and Other Preachings*, 69–78. Boston: Beacon, 2012.

————. "Minutes of the National Advisory Committee" [1967]. In *Bearing the Cross: Martin Luther King, Jr., and the Southern Christian Leadership Conference* by David J. Garrow. New York: HarperCollins, 2004.

————. "My Pilgrimage to Nonviolence" [1958]. In *The Papers of Martin Luther King, Jr., Volume IV: Symbol of the Movement, January 1957–December 1958*, edited by Clayborne Carson, Susan Carson, Adrienne Clay, Virginia Shadron, and Kieran Taylor, 475–477. Berkeley: University of California Press, 2000.

————. "My Trip to the Land of Gandhi" [1959]. In *"A Single Garment of Destiny": A Global Vision of Justice*, edited by Lewis V. Baldwin, 100–109. Boston: Beacon, 2012.

————. "National Labor Leadership Assembly for Peace, Chicago, Illinois, November 11, 1967." In *"All Labor Has Dignity,"* edited by Michael K. Honey, 137–152. Boston: Beacon, 2011.

————. "A New Sense of Direction" [1968]. *Worldview* (April 1972): 5–12.

————. "Notecards on Books of the Old Testament" [1953]. In *The Papers of Martin Luther King, Jr., Volume II: Rediscovering Precious Values, July 1951–November 1955*, edited by Clayborne Carson and Peter H. Holloran, 164–167. Berkeley: University of California Press, 1994.

————. "The Octopus of Poverty" [1965]. In *"A Single Garment of Destiny": A Global Vision of Justice*, edited by Lewis V. Baldwin, 118–119. Boston: Beacon, 2012.

————. "The Other America" [April 14, 1967]. https://diva.sfsu.edu/collections/sfbatv/bundles/191473.

————. "The Other America" [March 10, 1968]. In *"All Labor Has Dignity,"* edited by Michael K. Honey, 153–166. Boston: Beacon, 2011.

———. "'A Realistic Look at the Question of Progress in the Area of Race Relations,' Address Delivered at St. Louis Freedom Rally [10 April 1957]." In *The Papers of Martin Luther King, Jr., Volume VI: Advocate of the Social Gospel, September 1948–March 1963*, edited by Clayborne Carson, 167–179. Berkeley: University of California Press, 2007.

———. "Remaining Awake Through a Great Revolution" [1968]. In *A Knock at Midnight: Inspiration from the Great Sermons of Reverend Martin Luther King, Jr.*, edited by Clayborne Carson and Peter Holloran, 201–224. New York: Warner Books, 2000.

———. "Retail, Wholesale and Department Store Union (RWDSU) District 65" [1962]. In *"All Labor Has Dignity,"* edited by Michael K. Honey, 55–64. Boston: Beacon, 2011.

———. "Southern Christian Leadership Conference: A Proposal for the Development of a Nonviolent Action Movement in the Greater Chicago Area, 1966." In *The Civil Rights Movement: A Documentary Reader*, edited by John A. Kirk, 187–188. New York: Wiley, 2020.

———. "Speech at SCLC Staff Retreat" [1966]. The Archives of the King Center for Nonviolent Social Change, Atlanta, GA.

———. "Speech at SCLC Staff Retreat" [1967]. https://kairoscenter.org/mlk-frogmore -staff-retreat-speech-anniversary/.

———. "Speech to Mass Meeting: Edward, Mississippi" [1968]. In Sylvie Laurent, *King and the Other America: The Poor People's Campaign and the Quest for Economic Equality*, 171. Oakland: University of California Press, 2019.

———. "Statement on the Poor People's Campaign, December 4, 1967." The Archives of the King Center for Nonviolent Social Change, Atlanta, GA.

———. *Strength to Love*. 1963. Minneapolis, MN: Fortress Press, 2010.

———. *Stride Toward Freedom: The Montgomery Story*. 1958. Boston: Beacon, 2010.

———. "A Testament of Hope" [1969]. In *A Testament of Hope: The Essential Writings of Martin Luther King, Jr.*, edited by James. M. Washington, 313–328. New York: Harper and Row, 1986.

———. "Thirteenth Convention, United Packinghouse Workers of America, Minneapolis, Minnesota, May 21, 1962." In *"All Labor Has Dignity,"* edited by Michael K. Honey, 47–54. Boston: Beacon, 2011.

———. "The Three Dimensions of a Complete Life" [1976]. In *The Measure of a Man*, 37–52. Minneapolis: Augsburg Fortress, 2001.

———. "The Three Evils of Society, Address Delivered at the National Conference on New Politics, Chicago, Illinois, August 31, 1967." https://www.scribd.com/doc /134362247/Martin-Luther-King-Jr-The-Three-Evils-of-Society-1967.

———. "To C. L. R. James" [April 30, 1957]. https://kinginstitute.stanford.edu/king -papers/documents/c-l-r-james.

———. "To Minister to the Valley" [February 23, 1968]. Southern Christian Leadership Conference records, Stuart A. Rose Manuscript, Archives, and Rare Book Library, Emory University.

———. "To the Mountaintop" [1968]. In *"All Labor Has Dignity,"* edited by Michael K. Honey, 179–195. Boston: Beacon, 2011.

———. *The Trumpet of Conscience.* 1968. Boston: Beacon, 2000.

———. "United Automobile Workers Union, Detroit, Michigan, April 17, 1961." In *"All Labor Has Dignity,"* edited by Michael K. Honey, 23–30. Boston: Beacon, 2011.

———. *Where Do We Go from Here: Chaos or Community?* 1968. Boston: Beacon, 2010.

———. "Where Do We Go from Here?" [1967]. In *A Testament of Hope: The Essential Speeches and Writings of Martin Luther King, Jr.*, edited by James M. Washington, 245–252. New York: HarperOne, 2003.

———. "Will Capitalism Survive" [1951]. In *The Papers of Martin Luther King, Jr., Volume VI: Advocate of the Social Gospel, September 1948–March 1963*, edited by Clayborne Carson, 104–105. Berkeley: University of California Press, 2007.

Laurent, Sylvie. *King and the Other America: The Poor People's Campaign and the Quest for Economic Equality.* Oakland: University of California Press, 2018.

Le Blanc, Paul. "Martin Luther King: Christian Core, Socialist Bedrock." *Against the Current* 96 (January–February, 2002). https://solidarity-us.org/atc/96/p1030/.

Levine, David P. "The Birth of the Citizenship Schools: Entwining the Struggles for Literacy and Freedom." *History of Education Quarterly* 44, no. 3 (2004): 388–414.

Levinson, Marc. *An Extraordinary Time: The End of the Postwar Boom and the Return of the Ordinary Economy.* New York: Basic Books, 2016.

Lipsitz, George. "What Is This Black in the Black Radical Tradition?" In *Futures of Black Radicalism*, edited by Gaye Theresa Johnson and Alex Lubin, 108–119. New York: Verso, 2018.

Livingston, James. "Against Apocalypse Economics." *New Republic*, November 18, 2016. https://newrepublic.com/article/138809/apocalypse-economics.

———. *No More Work: Why Full Employment is a Bad Idea.* Chapel Hill: University of North Carolina Press, 2016.

Lloyd, Vincent W. *Black Natural Law.* New York: Oxford University Press, 2016.

Long, Michael G. *Against Us, But for Us: Martin Luther King, Jr. and the State.* Macon, GA: Mercer University Press, 2002.

Luxemburg, Rosa. *The Accumulation of Capital.* 1913. Translated by Agnes Schwarzschild. New York: Routledge, 2003.

Malcolm X. "The Harlem 'Hate-Gang' Scare" [1964]. In *Malcolm X Speaks: Selected Speeches and Statements*, edited by George Breitman, 64–71. New York: Grove Press, 1994.

Mantena, Karuna. "Showdown for Nonviolence: The Theory and Practice of Nonviolent Politics." In *To Shape a New World: Essays on the Political Philosophy of Martin Luther King, Jr.*, edited by Tommie Shelby and Brandon M. Terry, 78–101. Cambridge, MA: Harvard University Press, 2018.

Marable, Manning. *How Capitalism Underdeveloped Black America: Problems in Race, Political Economy, and Society.* 1983. Cambridge, MA: South End Press, 2000.

Marasco, Robyn. *The Highway of Despair: Critical Theory after Hegel*. New York: Columbia University Press, 2015.

Martel, James. "Stages of Freedom." *Black Perspectives*, June 14, 2016. https://www .aaihs.org/stages-of-freedom/.

Marx, Karl. *Capital: A Critique of Political Economy*. Vol. 1. 1867. Translated by Ben Fowkes. New York: Penguin, 1992 [1867].

——. *Capital: A Critique of Political Economy*. Vol. 2. 1885. Translated by David Fernbach. New York: Penguin, 1993.

——. *Capital: A Critique of Political Economy*. Vol. 3. 1894. Translated by David Fernbach. New York: Penguin, 1993.

——. *A Contribution to the Critique of Political Economy*. 1859. https://www.marxists .org/archive/marx/works/1859/critique-pol-economy/.

——. "Letter to Arnold Ruge" [1843]. Cited in Nancy Fraser, *Unruly Practices: Power, Discourse, and Gender in Contemporary Social Theory*. Second Edition, 113. Minneapolis: University of Minnesota Press, 2008.

——. "Marx on Slavery and the U.S. Civil War." Internationalist Group Class Readings, February 2008. https://www.marxists.org/history/etol/newspape /internationalist/pamphlets/MARX-on-Slavery-OptV5.pdf.

——. "Theories of Surplus Value" [1863]. https://www.marxists.org/archive/marx /works/1863/theories-surplus-value/ch17.htm.

Marx, Karl, and Friedrich Engels. *The Communist Manifesto*. 1848. New York: Penguin, 2002.

——. *The German Ideology*. 1845. Amherst, NY: Prometheus Books, 1998.

Mbembe, Achille. *Critique of Black Reason*. Translated by Laurent Dubois. Durham, NC: Duke University Press, 2017.

McWorter, Gerald. "The Nature and Needs of the Black University." *Negro Digest* 17, no. 5 (March 1968): 4–13.

Melamed, Jodi. "Racial Capitalism." *Critical Ethnic Studies* 1, no. 1 (Spring 2015): 76–85.

——. *Represent and Destroy: Rationalizing Violence in the New Racial Capitalism*. Minneapolis: University of Minnesota Press, 2011.

Meyerson, Gregory. "Rethinking Black Marxism: Reflections on Cedric Robinson and Others." *Cultural Logic* 3, no. 2 (Spring 2000): 1–48.

Moskowitz, Peter. "Meet the Radical Workers' Cooperative Growing in the Heart of the Deep South." *The Nation*, April 24, 2017. https://www.thenation.com/article /meet-the-radical-workers-cooperative-growing-in-the-heart-of-the-deep-south/.

Moyn, Samuel. "Welfare World." *Humanity: An international Journal of Human Rights, Humanitarianism, and Development* 1, no. 1. (2017): 175–183.

Myers, Joshua M. *We Are Worth Fighting For: A History of the Howard University Protest of 1989*. New York: New York University Press, 2019.

Myerson, Jesse A., and Mychal Denzel Smith. "We'll Need an Economic Program to Make #BlackLivesMatter: Here Are Three Ideas." *The Nation*, January 7, 2015. https://www.thenation.com/article/archive/economic-program-blacklivesmatter/.

Myrdal, Gunnar. *An International Economy: Problems and Prospects*. New York: Harper and Row, 1956.

Nadasen, Premilla. "'We Do Whatever Becomes Necessary': Johnnie Tillmon, Welfare Rights, and Black Power." In *Want to Start a Revolution: Radical Women in the Black Freedom Struggle*, edited by Dayo Gore, Jeanne Theoharis, and Komozi Woodard, 317–338. New York: New York University Press, 2009.

———. *Welfare Warriors: The Welfare Rights Movement in the United States*. New York: Routledge, 2005.

National Advisory Commission on Civil Disorders. *The Kerner Report*. 1968. Princeton, NJ: Princeton University Press, 2016.

New York Times Editorial Board. "Dr. King's Error." *New York Times*, April 7, 1967: 36.

Nkrumah, Kwame. *Consciencism: Philosophy and Ideology for De-colonization and Development with Particular Reference to the African Revolution*. New York: Monthly Review, 1964.

paperson, la. *A Third University Is Possible*. Minneapolis: University of Minnesota Press, 2017.

Payne, Charles M. *I've Got the Light of Freedom: The Organizing Tradition and the Mississippi Freedom Struggle*. 2nd ed. Berkeley: University of California Press, 2007.

Phillips, Christine. "In the latest JFK files: The FBI's ugly analysis on Martin Luther King Jr., filled with falsehoods." *Washington Post*, November 4, 2017. https://www.washingtonpost.com/news/retropolis/wp/2017/11/04/in-the-latest-jfk-files-the-fbis-ugly-analysis-on-martin-luther-king-jr-filled-with-falsehoods/?noredirect=on&utm_term=.dc5edea444fa (accessed August 2, 2018).

Poinsett, Alex. "Think Tank for Black Scholars: Institute of the Black World Serves Liberation Movement." *Ebony* 25, no. 4 (Feb. 1970): 46–54.

Quan, H. L. T. "'It's Hard to Stop Rebels That Time Travel': Democratic Living and the Radical Imagining of Old Worlds." In *Futures of Black Radicalism*, edited by Gaye Theresa Johnson and Alex Lubin, 173–193. New York: Verso, 2018.

Ralph, James, Jr. *Northern Protest: Martin Luther King, Jr., Chicago, and the Civil Rights Movement*. Cambridge, MA: Harvard University Press, 1993.

Ransby, Barbara. *Ella Baker and the Black Freedom Movement: A Radical Democratic Vision*. Chapel Hill: University of North Carolina Press, 2005.

Rasberry, Vaughn. *Race and the Totalitarian Century: Geopolitics in the Black Literary Imagination*. Cambridge: Harvard University Press, 2016.

Reed, Adolph, Jr. *Class Notes: Posing as Politics and Other Thoughts on the American Scene*. New York: The New Press, 2001.

———. "Introduction to Oliver C. Cox." In *Race: A Study in Social Dynamics: 50th Anniversary Edition of* Caste, Class, and Race, by Oliver Cromwell Cox, ix–xvii. New York: Monthly Review, 2000.

Rickford, Russell. *We Are an African People: Independent Education, Black Power, and the Radical Imagination*. New York: Oxford University Press, 2019.

Roberts, Michael. *The Long Depression: Marxism and the Global Crisis of Capitalism.* Chicago: Haymarket, 2016.

Roberts, Neil. "Theorizing Freedom, Radicalizing the Black Radical Tradition: On *Freedom as Marronage* Between Past and Future." *Theory & Event* 20, no. 1 (2017): 212–230.

Roberts, William Claire. *Marx's Inferno: The Political Theory of Capital.* Princeton, NJ: Princeton University Press, 2017.

Robinson, Cedric J. *Black Marxism: The Making of the Black Radical Tradition.* 1983. Chapel Hill: University of North Carolina Press, 2000.

———. *Black Movements in America.* New York: Routledge, 1997.

———. "In Search of a Pan-African Commonwealth." *Social Identities* 2, no. 1 (February 1996): 161–169.

———. "Notes toward a 'Native' Theory of History." *Review (Fernand Braudel Center)* 4, no. 1 (1980): 45–78.

———. *The Terms of Order: Political Science and the Myth of Leadership.* 1980. Chapel Hill: University of North Carolina Press, 2016.

Robinson, Cedric J., and Chuck Morse. "Capitalism, Marxism, and the Black Radical Tradition: An Interview with Cedric Robinson." *Perspectives on Anarchist Theory* 3, no. 1 (Spring 1999): 1–8.

Rodney, Walter. *The Groundings with My Brothers.* 1969. New York: Verso, 2019.

———. *How Europe Underdeveloped Africa.* 1973. Baltimore, MD: Black Classic Press, 2011.

———. *Walter Rodney Speaks: The Making of an African Intellectual.* Trenton, NJ: Africa World Press, 1990.

Rodriguez, Dylan. "The Political Logic of the Non-Profit Industrial Complex." In *The Revolution Will Not Be Funded: Beyond the Non-Profit Industrial Complex*, by INCITE! Women of Color against Violence, 21–40. Durham, NC: Duke University Press, 2017.

Roediger, David. *Class, Race, and Marxism.* New York: Verso, 2017.

———. *The Wages of Whiteness: Race and the Making of the American Working Class.* New York: Verso, 2007.

Scott, David. *Conscripts of Modernity: The Tragedy of Colonial Enlightenment.* Durham, NC: Duke University Press, 2004.

———. "On the Very Idea of a Black Radical Tradition." *Small Axe* 17, no 1. (2013): 1–6.

Scott King, Coretta. *My Life, My Love, My Legacy.* New York: Henry Holt, 2017.

Shelby, Tommie. "Prisons of the Forgotten: Ghettoes and Economic Injustice." In *To Shape a New World: Essays on the Political Philosophy of Martin Luther King, Jr.*, edited by Tommie Shelby and Brandon M. Terry, 187–204. Cambridge, MA: Harvard University Press, 2018.

Singh, Nikhil Pal. *Race and America's Long War.* Oakland: University of California Press, 2017.

Smallwood, Stephanie. "What Slavery Tells Us about Marx." *Boston Review* Forum 1: Race Capitalism Justice (Winter 2017). http://bostonreview.net/forum /remake-world-slavery-racial-capitalism-and-justice/stephanie-smallwood -what-slavery-tells-us.

Sokol, Jason. *There Goes My Everything: White Southerners in the Age of Civil Rights, 1945–1975.* New York: Vintage, 2007.

Spence, Lester K. *Knocking the Hustle: Against the Neoliberal Turn in Black Politics.* New York: Punctum Books, 2015.

Streeck, Wolfgang. *How Will Capitalism End?* New York: Verso, 2016.

Sundstrom, Ronald. "The Prophetic Tension between Race Consciousness and the Ideal of Colorblindness." In *To Shape a New World: Essays on the Political Philosophy of Martin Luther King, Jr.*, edited by Tommie Shelby and Brandon M. Terry, 127–145. Cambridge, MA: Harvard University Press, 2018.

Sustar, Lee. "The Evolution of Dr. King." *Jacobin,* January 16, 2017. https://www .jacobinmag.com/2017/01/martin-luther-king-socialist/.

Taylor, Keeanga-Yamahtta. *From #BlackLivesMatter to Black Liberation.* Chicago: Haymarket, 2016.

Terry, Brandon M. "Requiem for a Dream: The Problem-Space of Black Power." In *To Shape a New World: Essays on the Political Philosophy of Martin Luther King, Jr.*, edited by Tommie Shelby and Brandon M. Terry, 290–324. Cambridge, MA: Harvard University Press, 2018.

Theoharis, Jeanne. "'I Am Not a Symbol, I Am an Activist': The Untold Story of Coretta Scott King." *The Guardian*, February 3, 2018. https://www.theguardian .com/world/2018/feb/03/coretta-scott-king-extract.

Thompson, Heather Ann. *Blood in the Water: The Attica Prison Uprising of 1971 and Its Legacy.* New York: Pantheon, 2016.

Threadcraft, Shatema, and Brandon M. Terry. "Gender Trouble: Manhood, Inclusion, and Justice." In *To Shape a New World: Essays on the Political Philosophy of Martin Luther King, Jr.*, edited by Tommie Shelby and Brandon M. Terry, 205–235. Cambridge, MA: Harvard University Press, 2018.

Tillmon, Johnnie. "Welfare is a Women's Issue." *Ms. Magazine* 1, no. 1 (1972): 111–116.

Tully, James. *Public Philosophy in a New Key, Volume I: Democracy and Civic Freedom.* New York: Cambridge University Press, 2008.

Wang, Jackie. *Carceral Capitalism.* South Pasadena, CA: Semiotext(e), 2018.

Watson, Melvin. "Letter to King" [14 August, 1952], in *The Papers of Martin Luther King, Jr., Vol. II: Rediscovering Precious Values, July 1951–November 1955,* edited by Clayborne Carson and Peter H. Holloran, 156–157. Berkeley: University of California Press, 1994.

West, Cornel, ed. *The Radical King.* Boston: Beacon, 2015.

White, Derrick E. "Audacious Visions: The Intellectual-Activist Legacies of W. E. B. DuBois, the Institute of the Black World, and Walter Rodney." *South* 1, no. 1 (2015). https://digitalcommons.kennesaw.edu/south/vol1/iss1/4.

———. "Black Metamorphosis: A Prelude to Sylvia Wynter's Theory of the Human." *The CLR James Journal* 16, no. 1 (Spring 2010): 127–148.

———. *The Challenge of Blackness: The Institute of the Black World and Political Activism in the 1970s*. Gainesville: University Press of Florida, 2011.

———. "The Institute of the Black World and Atlanta as Black Intellectual Mecca in the 1970s." *Atlanta Studies*, October, 3, 2017. https://doi.org/10.18737/atls20171003.

Wilder, Craig Steven. *Ebony and Ivy: Race, Slavery, and the Troubled History of America's Universities*. New York: Bloomsbury, 2013.

Wilderson Frank, III. "Gramsci's Black Marx: Whither the Slave in Civil Society?" *Social Identities* 9, no. 2 (2003): 225–240.

Williams, Thomas D., and Jan Olof Bengtsson. "Personalism." In *Stanford Encyclopedia of Philosophy* (Summer 2016 edition), edited by Edward N. Zalta. Stanford University. Published November 12, 2009; last modified January 8, 2020. https://plato.stanford.edu/archives/sum2016/entries/personalism/.

Wynter, Sylvia. "Unsettling the Coloniality of Being/Power/Truth/Freedom: Towards the Human, After Man, Its Overrepresentation—An Argument." CR: The New Centennial Review 3, no. 3 (2003): 257–337.

INDEX

Akuno, Kali, 8–9, 104n51
Albany Movement, 39–40
Allen, Robert, 81–82, 85
Amin, Samir, 51, 107n87
antipolitical, 12, 63–64, 72–73. *See also*
  politics; Robinson, Cedric J.; state
automation, 8, 43

Baker, Ella, 38, 67, 76, 77–79
Baker, Houston, 20–21
Baldwin, Lewis, 20, 25–26, 31
Bandung Conference, 52, 89, 107n87.
  See also Global South
Baraka, Amiri, 1
Barber, William J., 71
Barbour, J. Pius, 36
Belafonte, Harry, 1–2
beloved community, 63–64; as Black
  study 75, 91; foreclosed by racial
  capitalism, 12, 37; and King's
  democratic vision, 14, 25–26, 32, 56;
  and mysticism, 69; and state, 109–
  110n38. *See also* Christianity
Bennett, Lerone, 76, 84
Berdyaev, Nikolai, 38–39
Berry, Mary Frances, 85
Bevel, James, 42
Black capitalism, 82–83
Black counterpublic, 14, 18, 23, 30–31,
  72, 75
Black internationalism, 14, 49–52, 61,
  106n72
Black Lives Matter, 2, 8
Black Power, 9, 51, 74, 86, 113–114n31

Black radical tradition, 3, 9–12, 14, 15,
  56; and Afropessimism, 92; Edwards
  on, 31–32; as epistemology, 67–71; and
  Institute of the Black World, 77, 80;
  and James, 23–34; as ontology, 65–67;
  as resistance, 39, 45, 62–64. *See also*
  Christianity; Robinson, Cedric J.
Black social gospel, 68, 97n11. *See also*
  Christianity
Black studies, 15, 75–76, 83, 85–86,
  89–93, 115n48
Black university concept, 85–86, 89,
  115n63
Black working class, 9–10, 47, 50, 78, 82;
  and Black disposability, 44, 104n51;
  and Institute of the Black World, 75,
  82, 85; and King's upbringing, 20, 67,
  97n11; and welfare state, 58, 62. *See also*
  labor; organized labor; poverty
Boggs, James, 90
Bundy, McGeorge, 81–82
Burrow, Rufus, 25

Cabral, Amílcar, 85
capital accumulation, 5–9, 11, 13–14,
  34, 37–38, 40, 44–45, 51; and crisis,
  43–44, 49, 54; and dispossession,
  43, 104–105n53; primitive
  accumulation, 5–6, 47; and university,
  87–88. *See also* inequality; profit
  motive; property
capitalist value-form, 13–14, 30, 33–35,
  91, 101n4; and devaluation, 41–44,
  102–103n33; and state violence, 50–51.

131

violence (*continued*)
    distinction between people and
    property, 53; primitive accumulation,
    5–6, 47; state-sanctioned, 2, 57,
    109–110n38; war, 49–51. *See also*
    nonviolence; riots

wagelessness, 44, 50, 104n51; surplus
    population, 8, 43–44, 53
Wang, Jackie, 8
war, 49–51. *See also* violence
War on Poverty, 49, 57. *See also* poverty
Watson, Melvin, 39
welfare state, 14, 71, 109–110n38; and
    gendered capitalism, 58–59; global

dimensions of, 60–63, 109n18; and
    state-managed capitalism, 55–56,
    59–60, 70; and welfare rights
    activism, 57–58, 63, 67. *See also*
    governability; state
White, Derrick, 15, 76, 85, 113–114n31
Wilderson, Frank, 100n51
Wiley, George, 57
Wright, Richard, 3–4
Wynter, Sylvia, 76, 99n38, 115n71

X, Malcolm, 9

Young, Andrew, 1–2
Young Negroes' Cooperative League, 77

THE MOREHOUSE COLLEGE
KING COLLECTION
SERIES ON CIVIL & HUMAN RIGHTS

The Drum Major Instinct: Martin Luther King Jr.'s Theory of Political Service,
by Justin Rose

Reclaiming the Great World House: The Global Vision of Martin Luther King Jr.,
edited by Vicki L. Crawford and Lewis V. Baldwin

Dr. Martin Luther King Jr. and the Poor People's Campaign of 1968,
by Robert Hamilton

*Prophet of Discontent: Martin Luther King Jr. and
the Critique of Racial Capitalism,*
by Andrew J. Douglas and Jared A. Loggins

CPSIA information can be obtained
at www.ICGtesting.com
Printed in the USA
LVHW100754010222
709936LV00015B/2007